Against All Odds

Against All Odds

CALVIN AND LEANNE DAVIDSON

StoryTerrace

Text Zoe Apostolides, on behalf of StoryTerrace
Design StoryTerrace
Copyright © Calvin and Leanne Davidson

First print December 2022

StoryTerrace

www.StoryTerrace.com

CONTENTS

1.	HOW IT ALL BEGAN	7
2.	A CLOUD DESCENDS	15
3.	BOUNTY BEGINS – ONWARDS AND UPWARDS	33
4.	LEANNE PART 1	47
5.	LEANNE PART 2	55
6.	CALVIN PART 1	67
7.	CALVIN PART 2	77
8.	MEETING AND MARRIAGE	91
9.	COBI	123
10.	CHALLENGES	159
11.	LESSONS LEARNED AND FINAL THOUGHTS	183

1
HOW IT ALL BEGAN

Imagine the scene. The screen lights up, the button's flashing, you click, and you're in. Within seconds, you're directed to a web page. You wait. The seconds tick down. Suddenly, two faces appear, smiling. You've seen them before, and last time, there was a baby with them; now, however, a toddler is happily playing in the background and a dog's trying to knock the camera over. Maybe he'll succeed.

The draw begins. The man and woman on the screen are announcing numbers, prizes, winners. You continue to wait, fingers crossed, palms sweating. The minutes stretch into hours, it feels like. And then the house is announced – the house you bid on, the ticket you bought. You know the odds, and you've allowed yourself to hope . . . It's been a tough few months. Rising prices, petrol gone mad, food becoming too expensive and the car needing service. Yesterday, the boiler sounded like it was on the out. Just your luck.

And then they say it, and it's almost like they're speaking a different language. The man is laughing as he tells the audience, all of whom are watching at home, that the name of the winner is you.

You've won a house.

Every week, on Mondays, Wednesdays and Fridays, we change lives. We sit before our computer, drawing the lots and announcing prizes that range in value, from kettles and toasters to spa breaks, mini breaks, cars, houses, cash. Our screens provide the interactive element: we'll go live via our streaming app and speak through our microphones, reading our customer comments and responding to them. We probably draw around 30 prizes on Monday and Wednesday and 40 on Friday. These are long sessions, often lasting hours, but it's worth it.

Bounty Competitions is our business, our way of life, but it's not something we'd ever have imagined doing 15, 10 or even five years ago. Sometimes we still have to pinch ourselves, take a minute to reflect and remind ourselves that it really is happening, that this is us. You hear about entrepreneurs in the media or on TV shows like *Dragon's Den*: sure of themselves and their place in the world. They've been raised to think they will succeed, that their ventures will work out, that money will be made. They have confidence gained from years of accomplishment. And if for whatever reason, something goes wrong, they have safety nets, ways of getting out of the difficulty. Who knows, they might even start again. If I fail at first, they think, just try again – fail better.

We took that mindset on board – we both dropped out of school early and, in actual fact, didn't do super well academically, but we knew we needed confidence. And that's what we've now found.

As we write this, it's spring 2022. People are travelling again, and we're right there with them. The world is opening up once more. We live in Turriff, a town in Aberdeenshire; it's about an hour's drive south to get to the city. It's a lovely town, quiet and agricultural, but our house is a good way from our neighbours': it's a proper country life. If you drive 20 minutes or so by car, you'll come to the seaside resort of Banff and the chilly waters of the North Sea. When we're not working or visiting friends and family, we love exploring the local area, taking our dogs Bo and Lola out for long walks, soaking it all up. It's rural, and that's just the way we like it – this is proper Scottish weather, at times all rain and thunder, and at others glorious sunshine. A bit like life, really.

Our son, Cobi, turned three in January. We want to work hard to give Cobi the best possible upbringing and show him everything we have learned since starting Bounty. He will grow up knowing the value of hard graft. Hopefully when Cobi grows up he will use the skills we have taught him to start his own business.

Our weeks vary, of course, but generally, after completing

the draws, we'll spend the following day contacting winners. We have family working for us, and friends, and they will phone those who've won, get their addresses and contact details and enable us to start the deliveries. We'll personally deliver everything, unless the winner lives a good way away. Calvin's nephew Dale is our customer-service guru, and he'll deal with all enquiries while we're out, sometimes for as long as 10 or 12 hours. Calvin's sister Karen assists Dale and manages Bounty Holiday Lets.

These deliveries are important to us as they're a means to get to know a customer, speak with them, hear about how their prize will affect their lives, This is where our new assistant Brett really helps. Sometimes we're delivering cheques, sometimes cars. The DPD delivery drivers who drop the prizes off in the first place have become our best friends: most days, we'll have around £10,000 worth of tech gadgets leaving their vans and going into our custom-built holding space. As you can imagine, we have seriously tight security here, with cameras pointing in every direction. We're not sure how much use Bo and Lola would be in an emergency; they'd probably lick you to death.

Around the draws and the deliveries, we have the marketing to do, the Facebook and other social media posts to create, the emails and texts to respond to. It's a constant stream of updates, choices to be made, communications to be dealt with. As you can imagine, we meet with our accountant fairly regularly! We'll take our bank statements, our receipts, everything. We need that support – all businesses do. And we do things properly, making sure no stone is left unturned. You can't afford to be sloppy when you're dealing with this size of business.

We also own a holiday-let business, which Leanne started. Those homes will need occasional seeing-to, whether it's changing the water in a hot tub or fixing a technical issue. It's a separate business entirely from Bounty, but it means we don't have all our eggs in one basket. It's important to ensure a diverse portfolio of income streams – but it also means we're almost permanently knackered. People often ask us where we find the energy, and in some ways, we don't know. We just do. It helps that we have different skill sets, different strengths, and that we complement one another temperamentally. After all, we own and run a business together, but we're also husband and wife, as well as parents to Cobi.

We want this book to chart our journey and paint a picture of how we came to be where we are. We want to set it all down, explain the process of developing our business, give a sense of what it means to us. But we also want to dig deeper than that, to tell you a bit about our lives – both before we met and afterwards. We want to show you that anything is possible and that backgrounds don't matter. With the right skill set and the right attitude, it is possible to achieve success. We want this to be an informative but inspiring read. We'll describe our beginnings, our challenges, the problems we've faced, our meeting and marriage, the birth of our son – and how we manage and blend it all with work. We're going to be honest, open and transparent – no holds barred. We hope you enjoy coming along for the ride.

Bounty's Unit - The best it has ever looked!

Winner Michelle won our third house!

Winner Lee Jenson - Lee won our second house in Inverurie

2

A CLOUD DESCENDS

What would life be like today if it weren't for Bounty? If we'd never decided to take the plunge, to give it a go, to try even if we failed? It gives us both a chill to realise how easily our day-to-day could have stayed as it was. We'd be struggling now, no doubt about it, with all the rising energy, food and petrol costs, on top of the expense of having a child and wanting the absolute best for him.

Calvin

Prior to Covid, Leanne had paid to do several extra hairdressing courses and qualifications, and had barely taken a moment to breathe throughout her pregnancy. Every day, she was off, out the door, cutting and styling across Aberdeen city centre. Leanne made around £200 a week. We realised quickly that as working parents, bringing in two sets of wages and somehow finding a way to pay for nursery was going to be very challenging, even with the child benefit payment of £80 a month. Nowadays, Cobi goes in on Tuesdays, Wednesdays and Thursdays between 9 a.m. and 4 p.m., and that's £650 a month. Without a change in our jobs, we'd have been spending most of the monthly salary on childcare before bills, mortgage or rent payments and food were considered.

Boots the chemist, Debenhams, car salesperson jobs, everything: we applied for it all, anything for a bit of extra money. Meanwhile, we worked 12-hour days trying to make ends meet. I had helped build the events complex in Aberdeen as a labourer, and I had an NVQ in joinery. I was a hard worker, and my supervisors had seen potential in me. Getting my forklift licence saw my pay increase to £20 an hour, but I was depressed. I was surrounded by people who were also unhappy and feeling down, each one looking for a better way of life.

When Leanne fell pregnant, one of my colleagues at the construction site had been following her posts on Instagram. Very sadly, we lost our first baby, and when I got into work, that same colleague – whose wife was also pregnant – turned to me and said, smiling, 'At least my partner's still pregnant.'

I was totally shocked; it was so uncalled for. I was so angry I could have hit him, but of course, violence isn't the answer. Why on earth would he say something like that? I reported him to my good friend, Andy Jones, who was the supervisor. It didn't seem to stop the colleague, who'd post sly memes aimed at me in our group chats online and even went as far as telling me he'd seen Leanne out with another guy. I would have kept going in construction, surrounded by the likes of him, if it was likely to help my family. But it was making me depressed. Something had to give.

Our lives in March 2020 couldn't have been more different to how they are now. We were living in cramped conditions in Leanne's former flat, the two of us, and Cobi, plus Lola the dog. I hated my job, and though Leanne didn't mind hers, clients were beginning to get nervous about the close contact required for hair-cutting.

Eleven years prior to the pandemic, swine flu had caused similar panic in the media. For a few weeks, it was all anyone could talk about, and to be honest, in the first weeks of 2020, we felt the same. As January turned to February, strange reports were coming out of China – reports that were becoming increasingly hard to ignore. People were getting really sick, and some were dying. When the virus made its way to Italy, we saw with horror what it was doing to a healthcare system not so very different from our own. We saw the people on ventilators, doctors and nurses in tears, everyone in protective clothing and masks everywhere you looked. Suddenly, we could see that this was no swine flu.

March rolled around, and we braced ourselves for what was coming our way. I think, by the time the 23rd arrived, we knew we were headed for the same sort of lockdown we'd seen across Europe. We knew we were for it. But how on earth was anyone going to survive? How were people going to manage, go to work, earn a living? In some ways, we ignored it because the alternative was too hideous to imagine. We had a young child, a baby just 14 months old, and if one of us lost our income stream, we didn't know how we'd feed him properly. Leanne was told first that she needed to stop working: all hair and beauty salons were the first to be hit. For a time, then, we relied solely on one salary. We knew the grants – or the furlough scheme – was coming, but we didn't know when, we didn't know if we'd be entitled to it, and we didn't know how much, if anything, we were entitled to.

We were not only worried about money – the virus itself was concerning. No one had a clue, back then, what we were headed towards. It seemed like a deadly bug, and so we were torn between the desire to put food on the table and the need to protect ourselves and our loved ones. The lads at work had slowly stopped saying it was just Swine Flu 2.0, and then here it was, Coronavirus, on the shores of Britain.

'Sorry, lads,' said our manager one day. 'You need to stop work and go home.'

Everyone stared at him. He looked apologetic but just as confused as the rest of us. 'We can't keep the site open. Everywhere has to shut.'

'But how are we supposed to work – how are we going to survive?' someone asked.

The manager shrugged. 'I honestly don't know.'

Everything was looking like it couldn't really get any worse. And then the Prime Minister officially announced the end of life as we'd known it; suddenly, our lives changed forever. Never in the history of the country have its people been asked to stay home in this way before. No one knew what to do or how to react. We woke up feeling terrified, nervous, anxious about the future. How could it be that just 10 weeks prior, we'd been enjoying New Year's Eve? For a few days, we were both close to despair.

It's terrible not working. We all moan about our jobs from time to time, of course, but the reality of having no work is actually worse. Waking up and knowing you need to stay home, that the day will be exactly the same as yesterday, that you have no money coming in – it's torture. Neither of us worked in industries that allowed remote working. We couldn't log on at a certain time, do what we needed to via Zoom or Skype. Our jobs required physical presence, required us to be there.

Leanne

Calvin had recently achieved site-supervisor level, which meant more money; I had returned to work full-time after Cobi was 10 weeks old. We gave him the best life we could, but we were always in overdraft. We'd look out at the salon built in the garden and wonder how we were going to make ends meet: this building, crafted with such time and love and dedication, was now technically illegal to use except between the three of us, our so-called 'bubble'. To build it, Calvin had asked his manager for permission to take certain bits and bobs home from the site, spare parts that were no longer needed.

For a year before the lockdown, this is where I worked. My mum or Calvin's would come to babysit while I was outside, and at lunchtime, I'd be able to come in and see the baby. Calvin was always at work, it seemed. Most of the day and some of the night, in fact – from about 7 a.m. until nine some evenings. He'd gone back to work the very day after Cobi was born: as a self-employed father now, the new family just couldn't afford to lose £130 a day. I think Calvin was determined to provide for Cobi and myself – and he did. We went to Paphos in Cyprus and to Tenerife. It was all about the memories, even when money was really tight. And I'm grateful that we've always understood the huge value of family life: Cobi spent lots of time with both his grannies, which is so important to us.

Calvin

Nonetheless, for a long time, I had liked the idea of starting a competition business. There was so much about it that appealed to me – it was client-facing, and it involved draws where the business owners could interact with their customers and prizes that made people happy and gave them the same flutter and sense of anticipation as a day at the races. What was more, it could be done from home. Leanne wasn't on board initially. 'It'll never work, Calvin,' she sighed. 'I don't see how it can be financially viable.'

If Covid hadn't arrived, it's very likely I'd have started working offshore. I'd asked Leanne's stepdad for help previously, since he's a big offshore manager. He told me not to waste the £2,500 on offshore survival training as I wouldn't get any work. I was ready to go at a moment's notice to work miles from home. Anything to put food on the table and ensure a better quality of life for all three of us.

For a little while, we started a sort of raffles page – people would pay for tickets via PayPal, and we'd offer things like kettles, toasters and televisions. We were making around £10 per prize, which wasn't too bad because £50 equalled five large tubs of milk for the baby. It was fine, good business, but it wasn't enough. And if anyone complained about us, which they eventually did, we would be shut down. We not only had to start from scratch, but we needed to learn about the legality of what we were doing.

So many new competition businesses inadvertently break the law – they have no intention of doing so, but the wrong mistakes at the wrong time can lead to a complete breakdown of a business before it's even got off the ground. We have always strived to make sure that we do not make these same mistakes, so we ensure that Bounty complies with all necessary regulations. Prize competitions like ours aren't gambling, but you need to be careful. Businesses can be fined or shut down entirely if they don't comply with the laws, which says that to avoid being an illegal lottery, entrants must show 'sufficient' skill, knowledge or judgement to be in with a chance of winning. As an alternative, you can rely on an exemption to the Act, which asks multiple-choice questions and a fair way to enter for everyone.

Thankfully, one can also fall into the 'game of chance' category – games like Spot the Ball, for instance, rely on knowledge of football. These aren't games of skill, so they can't be defined as a lottery or a raffle. We quickly learned that if we used the wrong terminology, however innocently, the relevant bodies would be on to us in a flash: in fact, they called dozens of times in the early days, correcting and warning us of the consequences.

Since the sad death of Leanne's dad, we used the last of some inheritance money – not something we expected to do so early on. Soon enough, we were budgeting on everything. Money coming in was going out just as fast, and most of it was being spent on Cobi.

She'd worked hard beforehand, Leanne, and knew what sort of input an online retail business required. She did everything: make-up tutorials, for instance, were quite popular, and she developed a good-sized following there.

She'd obviously run her own hairdressing business, using her creativity and artistic side to build a good reputation. Even today, her interest in aesthetics means we have a booming property-let business, in addition to Bounty. At this stage, Leanne had also tried a clothing boutique that, in her own words, 'went down like a lead balloon'. Without significant money or marketing behind it, there was no way to get the word out, and although she sold a couple of dresses, the profit margin was about £2 an item – not nearly enough to start doing it to scale.

For a little while, we also tried a photo booth business, too – both sick and tired of our jobs, we looked into setting up something that actively made people happy. This seemed the perfect way – here we'd be selling the photo booth for hire at weddings and big, joyful events – it sounded good in principle, but after a while, for various reasons, we realised it wasn't working.

Clearly, the entrepreneurial spirit was there, though. By this point, in the earliest days of lockdown when everyone was buying online, Leanne had started network marketing, selling Ann Summers products, and, after doing some live videos promoting the clothes in question, hundreds of customers went on to buy. Mystery bags were flying off the shelves, and she had her own Facebook group dedicated to the work, which brought in £30 a week. 'Look,' I said to her, 'We can obviously do this for ourselves. You're doing it so well here already – but we can do it on our own steam.'

Leanne said yes – it was an important moment for us.

The moment we'd decided to do it, we got on the phone with Calvin's friend Anton. Our original plan was for a company called Lucky Lockdown Prizes – it was Anton, actually, who suggested that since we wanted the business to continue past the lockdowns, it'd be better not to reference Covid and instead try to come up with a name that reflected something longer lasting. After a few chats and back and forth, it was Leanne who came up with the name we both liked and which stuck. Bounty was born.

It's funny because Anton really had no idea what a competition business was, but he was a skilled web page designer. He started designing our first website for us, and he'll be the first to admit, I'm sure, that it had loads of flaws, but it was a start. Our first-ever listed prize was a Shark hoover. It's such a far cry from today, when we have three draws a week, each with a variety of prizes. Back then, our ethos was slowly, slowly: we didn't rush anything.

So, how does it work? It's quite simple, really. Each ticket costs a certain amount, and there are a certain amount of tickets available, depending on what the item is. The website lists many different competitions at once, everything from a Dyson hairdryer to half a million pounds in cash. The hairdryer would have a lower-entry cost, for example, perhaps just 99p, whereas to enter the draw for half a million might cost £9.99 per ticket. The odds and the ticket prices are both fair. Once you've selected, there's a simple check-out process online, and then the waiting – until the live draw – begins.

What we've created here had a one in six million chance of success. That's the number of people here in Scotland. Understandably, so many people wanted to make a difference and try something else during lockdown – so many whose jobs were totally ruined or finished altogether and who needed to find a new solution.

There are two main reasons we do what we do. We have an intense desire and passion to change lives – and that is exactly what the business does. No matter how big or small the prize is, a customer has decided to purchase a ticket because that prize is something they otherwise wouldn't be able to afford, or which would completely change their lives as a one-off cash lump sum.

When we earned a certain amount, we decided to invest in a proper, custom-built website. Each decision like this was exciting, of course, but also terrifying. We wanted the business to grow, but at the same time, we were scared that the next step, the next big turning point, would prove the end of Bounty. Were we stretching too far? Were we pushing ourselves too soon? What happened if we invested more money and it didn't work? We'd have lost it all.

As it happened, the new website saw us explode. No one had ever set up a competition business in the north of Scotland, and it was clear we'd captured the market. At one stage, we were flabbergasted to discover that 10,000 people were watching our live draws. Many families, couples or single people were sat at home with nothing to do, it seemed, and spare money to spend. When we drove to drop off prizes at a social distance, people cheered us from their doorsteps. It worked out so well from a lockdown perspective because, obviously, we could work primarily from home – but we were also allowed to work as delivery drivers. Our slogan – 'Hell yeah!' – became more and more widely known and used. Suddenly, cars would slow when they saw us coming up the road, and people we'd never met would wind down their windows to call out to us. It felt like being famous, and to be honest, the novelty still hasn't worn off.

We didn't anticipate the business to grow as fast as it did. But things snowballed, either through word-of-mouth, through our marketing campaigns, or from our own hard work. We're so grateful to our customers for wanting to join the journey, and we want everyone to know that we absolutely do not take what's happened for granted. It still doesn't feel real to look into the unit and see a Lamborghini parked there. When we test drive the prizes, we quite often turn to one another and smile. How did this happen to us? We imagine this sense of disbelief won't ever truly leave us.

Once Bounty was established, we knew we needed to take some financial advice to ensure we were ready and that our assets were protected. We were entirely self-made, but no one had ever explained how not only to make money but to spend and save it wisely. We're very careful with what we spend our money on. Investing in holiday lets seemed a natural next option – a way of diversifying our money and ensuring that we invested in something that wouldn't lose value, such as property.

No one gave us any money, and we've had to work for everything we have. It wasn't inherited or handed to us on a plate. For years, we'd wondered, both separately and together, when our luck was going to change. We looked for opportunities, we did the best we could with our skills, talents and education, and we kept in mind that a successful business would change not only our lives but other people's, too.

Calvin working in construction

The first pregnancy test we took in Greece, pregnant with Cobi

Calvin building the home salon

The old flat in Buckburn (ground floor) where Bounty began!

Our first new year together (in the middle of renovating the flat!)

3

BOUNTY BEGINS – ONWARDS AND UPWARDS

'It'll never work.'
'Trust me; we can do it. We just have to give it a try.'
'It's a lot of money, Calvin. We have to be sure.'
'I know, I get it. But we won't have any chance of succeeding if we don't try.'
'So, what next?'

These conversations went round and round. We'd discuss the pros and cons, the potential pitfalls, the challenges we were likely to face. While Calvin had been toying with the idea of a competition business for the past three years, Leanne needed a bit more convincing. But now it was lockdown, and we were both out of work. Once a day, we were permitted to walk outside with our newborn baby, discussing the business plan, the way it would work, the design, the logo, the name. But we needed to take the plunge.

Contacting Anton was the first step. He agreed to help us design a good-looking website for the company, and the next decision was the name. On the very morning that we went to register ourselves at Companies House, we'd originally agreed on a different name. It turned out that just two hours previously, an Irish company had registered that exact name. A competitor, then. We later discovered that their business went under, and we've since wondered if the name had something to do with it. We went back to the drawing board, batting names back and forth between us. Trophy, pirate, raiders, rovers, rewards, prizes . . . we began to play with the theme of pirates, and it was then, as we suggested ideas to one another, that Leanne paused and said, 'Bounty?'

Bounty is a sum of money paid as a reward, a large amount of something, or a kindness, a willingness to give. For the first time, we both felt we'd hit on something there. It fit in every way we wanted it to. It sounded good, too – not like the other name. Bounty sounded honest, fun, approachable, relatable. We rang Anton, who immediately told us that was the best idea he'd heard so far. And this was where it all began, really. We had our name, and now we had our site.

We settled on black and yellow as our primary colours and created our logo, a trophy surrounded by a pair of white, leaf-like arms on the left and right. Our next task was to encourage people to buy tickets. All this time and effort, the investment in the site and branding, the 2010 Subaru car we'd purchased – it was nothing without customers actually deciding to jump on board. We'd launched the site now, and we were ready – but first, people needed to know who we were.

Understandably, and especially during lockdown, people were sceptical of new businesses. They were concerned that desperation might lead to a spike in crime, fraud, theft – all sorts, really. And being out of work did indeed put the fear of God into everyone, of course. It was right that early on, people were suspicious of new businesses – so many of them were springing up, and not all of them were legitimate. Suddenly, you had con artists pretending to be from the NHS, phoning vulnerable old people and getting them to part with cash in exchange for bogus 'testing kits'. You had complex, hard-to-intercept phone scams, hoax calls – all manner of rubbish.

To put minds at ease, we made sure to convince customers early. Our trademark, which continues to this day, was going live. We interacted with those watching our streams; we made jokes, bantered with one another and with the customers, and got to know them. We were determined not to fall at the first hurdle, to give this our all. Our first customers were mainly from Montrose, Brechin and Whitehaven, the three places Calvin had the most connections. Calvin was sharing our link on our personal Facebook pages, after all, so it made sense that the initial interest came from those we'd previously known, those who wanted to support a new business set up by a mate. This turned out to be key: we cracked the local market, and we branched out from there.

We had hundreds of people on our pages within a few weeks. It helped that we seemed to be in the same boat as those who were watching: tired, stressed, sad that we weren't able to see family and friends. We tried to make those early lives as upbeat and energetic as possible, and tried to ensure people felt a bit of joy when they logged on, even if they didn't necessarily win. We asked our customers how they were getting on, what they were doing with their days, and generally formed a rapport with them, introducing them to our business and way of working.

Since we were able to deliver winners' prizes, we started taking our winners' banner and large novelty cheques out with us, taking pictures of winners with their prizes, to show that we were absolutely legitimate. This was instrumental because the snowball effect really started there. Word of mouth spread like wildfire, and we had the proof positive – through live streams and photos – that the prizes were genuine. Not only that, but they were getting better all the time, from hairdryers to hoovers and then cars, houses and huge cash prizes. It still seems incredible that we've now had almost 10,000 winners to date.

Of course, it wasn't all smooth sailing – far from it. Those early days were spent sitting before a screen in a tiny city-centre flat – we didn't have proper cameras or microphones;

we didn't have the tech set up to show the winning numbers in real time. In fact, we barely had anything at all. When we moved to Ellon and started operating there, we had constant complaints from neighbours who were unhappy at all these new flashy cars which were prizes appearing on the street.

Every time we walked around the Teca event complex during those lockdown walks, we'd contemplate how Calvin had helped build it during his last job pre-Covid. We'd walk around there endlessly, discussing all these aspects of the business, trying to make the most of our time outdoors. We'd brainstorm, visualise what we had to do, make a loop of the complex and then head up to the forests with Lola the dog in the sports pram beside Cobi.

As the months went by, we began to realise how important it was to switch off, to ensure we remained both business partners and married partners, too. Of the pair of us, Leanne is better at this. Leanne's always saying not to get stressed, to take a deep breath and try to calm down. It can be difficult – at the weekends, we sometimes travel hours in a single day, visiting a winner and doing a live before driving back. We sometimes incorporate dropping off two prizes at the same time – a car in Blackburn, for instance, and a pair of sleek new watches in Stirling.

Every day is totally different, and while that stops things from becoming stale, the lack of routine can sometimes be tricky. We'll go from seeing the winner of a Mercedes C63 to picking up bar stools for one of our lodges, and then we'll head to another lodge for minor maintenance work based on guests' feedback. As well as these tasks, we'll organise our staff; do our live draws on Monday, Wednesday and Friday; see to the holiday lets; speak to cleaners; manage Cobi's nursery, social plans and activities and arrange for time to spend just the three of us – along with seeing our wider family, walking the dogs and more things besides than we can currently remember. We'll ask Brett, who works for us doing customer-service enquiries and deliveries, to take some deliveries on for us, and together we'll load up a trailer headed to Glasgow and drop another car off somewhere else, all the while trying to find and source the next round of prizes.

Some people seem to think we sit around all day doing nothing, but seriously, military operations would probably be easier than our day-to-day. We respond to emails, phone calls and letters; speak to our accountant and to solicitors; pay our staff; make lists; plan meetings and work around staff holidays or absences. Some days are incredibly stressful, but as more and more people join us and the load is spread more evenly, those days are becoming less frequent.

One of the most important things for us about the job is our ability to give back. We recently sponsored a fantastic local community event, T-Urra in the Park, which was a great few days of music – Scouting for Girls and Toploader being highlights – and a big marquee full of booze! In the past, we've sponsored a local boxer, too: charity starts at home, after all, and we're always more inclined to help if someone's known to us or we feel an empathy with the cause.

And since Bounty began in places we knew and loved and has branched out to include north-eastern Scotland more generally, we know we've changed lives in our local community. There's something very special about being able to tell someone he's won a holiday in Dubai worth £30,000, a holiday where for five nights, he'll be treated like absolute royalty. He'd never have spent that money on himself – who would, unless they were a multi-millionaire? – and when we give news like this, we can almost hear the customer shaking over the phone.

At Christmas, we tend to do a 'trolley dash' – we go into a toy shop or department store and pick up literally thousands of pounds' worth of toys and presents. We're not in work mode at times like this, and all we have in mind are the people who'll enjoy these gifts. Whether it's a sick child in hospital who might not recover, a family struggling to make ends meet or kids whose parents are on drugs and aren't doing well, it feels so good to be able to help now when we can. We want to make other people happy; it's a highlight for us, and we will always donate to charity.

We've raised £183,000 for charity to date, and we're aiming for £200,000 by the end of the year. These have ranged from children's charity to animal charities, some 100 different charities over the past years. There have been too many to name, some big and some small, but some stand out.

AGAINST ALL ODDS

Charlie House who we support and regularly donate to have given us the opportunity to sponsor their new car park at the respite centre. They support terminally ill children and their families, and they do some really excellent work across Scotland but are based in Aberdeen. We're also meeting with Bounty the guide dog soon: a black lab about whom we receive regular 'pupdates'. We paid for the dog's training and sponsored him, something that will be life-changing for whoever goes on to pair with him. He even looks like a Bounty. And we sent a little girl, who is terminally ill, to DisneyWorld, raising around £6,000 to fulfil her wish.

We donate a great deal to Aber Necessities, a charity that often needs buggies or travel cots – things for babies – and to which our customers will sometimes donate their prizes directly. We collect nappies and baby beds whenever we can – and having had a tour of the charity's premises, it's clear that it's for a worthy cause. A social worker told us they'd once had an application filled out for a cot by a household where the baby was sleeping on a dog bed. To date, we've probably donated a good £40,000 to this excellent cause. It's very close to our hearts, particularly because we could well have ended up in that situation ourselves. For a time, we didn't have a single penny to scrape the barrel with, and if it weren't for Covid, there's no doubt our lives would not be what they are today. We can really relate to these sorts of charities since we were almost in need of them ourselves not so long ago.

Just recently, we had our first £500,000 winner. Her name was Sheelagh, and she cried when we went to see her – cried uncontrollably. She told us how she'd been struggling recently, how this money would change her life. Our mics went down just as we were about to announce the winner – tech! – but when we video called her that day, we could see how much it meant to her. That's why we do what we do. We know now that one person's life has been completely transformed by what we've facilitated.

In addition to cars and cash prizes, our other big prizes are houses. We always offer £10,000 in addition to the house or its cash equivalent, and we always donate £10,000 to charity at the same time. To date, we've given away four houses – four places for people to live and make their own.

We recently had a huge celebration of Bounty, complete with DJs, bouncy castles, stalls, flowing alcohol and a huge firework display. Hundreds of people came, which was wonderful, and it was so nice to be able to put it on and celebrate. However, when we went live during the firework display, we experienced a backlash. Some people were saying we were wasteful, just firing money into the sky, saying that their baby had woken up or their dog was scared. It was just such a shame to think we'd gone to all this trouble and still there were haters, people who complained and moaned and saw the negative when all we wanted was to give the community a party.

It's times like this that let us know we need a little break

AGAINST ALL ODDS

– we'll take the time to go offline, to care for ourselves and our health, go for a walk, head to the garden centre, turn our phones off and play with Cobi. We'll reduce our alcohol intake, start working with our personal trainer again, and really try to decompress – sometimes somewhere really remote, like a bothy in the middle of nowhere. For a few days, we'll be off-grid, leaving the business to our wonderful team and knowing that it will continue to thrive if we do.

The living room where Bounty started

Bounty's first ever car prize!

In the living room where Bounty started – Halloween!

4
LEANNE PART 1

We all have a start in life, be it good or bad. I'm lucky enough to say that mine was excellent. My parents, Gillian and Raymond, did everything they could for me and my sister and ensured we never went without. We weren't rolling in money, but we never wanted for anything, really, and it was a happy, carefree sort of childhood. My parents had been together for some time when they got married, and then, in 1990, they had my elder sister, Emma. I wasn't planned, but I arrived four years later. We were now a family of four.

Emma and I were raised in Stonehaven – a town about 17 miles south of Aberdeen and not far from Scotland's northeastern beaches. It's only about 90 minutes by car from where I live now, in fact. For my first five years, we were in Hunter Place. My mum worked in the chemist – first for Boots and then at Michies in the town itself. She also did cleaning jobs – anything to bring in a bit of extra income. At one stage, she had three separate jobs. It must have been exhausting, but it was the norm in a way – wages were far lower back then than they are now.

My dad, Ray, left school with no qualifications and didn't have much education behind him. He worked on the Waltzers in his younger days – a proper carnie, he'd been with various funfairs as a teenager and had been quite rebellious, I think. Not long afterwards, he started doing boat mechanics along with his best friend, Peter, and went straight from this job to working offshore.

This was big business for many Scottish men, especially during the 1980s and 1990s. They'd go off for weeks at a time to be on these oil rigs, just like Dad did, and work in rotational patterns of four weeks – spending a month 'onshore' again after every posting. I think he had his own room, or he shared with just one or two others. There were day and night shifts for all the men – and it was hard work. Just six years before I was born, the Piper Alpha oil platform exploded and sank, killing 165 of the men on board. Everyone was aware of the risks, but the pay was decent, and it was a necessity. My dad also worked in Nigeria for a while, too – these rigs were mostly based out in the desert, though: a totally different working environment.

My parents always did their best when it came to our birthdays or Christmas. My sister was obsessed – as so many little girls were – with the Spice Girls, and I can still see the image of the green pillow she so proudly owned with the word SPICE emblazoned across it. One of my earliest memories dates back to the age of about four. There was a huge bouncy castle in the back garden, and Mum had drunk a little too much. She and her friend Elaine climbed along the thick bit of the bouncy castle, and Mum fell off, smashing and breaking her nose in the process. I can remember her running into the house surrounded by loads of kids at the party – there was blood everywhere, and my dad was in the midst of us, trying to keep us away from the bathroom where Mum had slammed the door. She'll hate me for telling that story!

I was five when my parents separated, and though I wished they hadn't, Emma and I were never shown any of the difficulties they must have been having prior to the split. We moved out of Hunter Place after that, and from then on, we spent weekends with my dad when he wasn't on the rig. It seemed to us, in fact, that they got on even better once the relationship broke down. And their example was a good one because even though they'd separated, they showed Emma and me that it was possible to work together, nonetheless.

I wouldn't say the fact of their divorce particularly upset me – I can't remember them telling me what had happened, for instance. Only that suddenly, we weren't all living in the same place. I think Dad had been badly behaved, to be honest – he was a bit of a flirt, and Mum caught on. She didn't tell me any of this until I was about 14, though, to her credit. They always seemed to keep things companionable between them, and they seemed keen for us not to take sides.

They both started dating quite soon after the break-up. I got used to them being with other people, but I can't say I liked it very much. And it proved an easy excuse if one of their partners asked – or told – me to do something. 'You're not my dad!' I'd shout back, and there wasn't much they could say about that really, was there? One of the hard elements of the break-up was the fact that Dad's girlfriend of about seven years had kids the same age as Emma and me. This hurt – I can remember the intense jealousy I felt knowing they saw him all the time, whereas, for us, it was only at the weekends. It didn't feel right. It was unfair. Although I can't say I was traumatically impacted by their break-up, I think that as a child, I had a deeper connection with Dad. I always – and will always – love my mum, but in terms of our personalities, me and Dad were the same. We loved cars, we had a fun sense of humour, and we loved taking the mick out of each other – we were like two proper peas in a pod.

Money became a bit more of an issue following our parents' separation, but we were always their top priority. When they were together, Mum had worked more in part-time roles, but now she was working round the clock. Our nice semi-detached bungalow was gone, and now Mum made do with her wages, child maintenance and graft. She'd finish at 2 p.m. at the chemists and go straight into cleaning people's houses or doing their ironing: she was always on the go. We moved with her into a council house, which was hard because the council paid no attention to the number of people being housed. We were given a two-bedroom flat, but the second room was a box, and as a result, Emma and I had to share a bed. Nonetheless, Mum saved, and within no time at all, she was able to buy an ex-council, three-bed, mid-terraced house in Stonehaven.

We moved into our new house when I was seven or eight, and it was here we experienced true freedom: playing on the beaches, walking into town or onto the shoreline at the weekends or after school. Things were safe for us: there was little crime, and we were at liberty to roam.

I don't think either of my parents especially liked each other's new partner. As we grew older, we suspected a level of antipathy on this subject and fuelled it slightly, reporting back to each parent on what the other's partner had said or done. In all honesty, I think it was fuelled primarily by regret – there was always going to be something between them, after all. They had two kids together and had been a couple long before we arrived. At one stage, the atmosphere between Emma and Dad became really bad, and in fact, she wouldn't speak to him for about two years. I can distinctly remember being about 10 and Dad jokingly asking if our mum would ever take him back. I knew it wasn't a serious question, but a part of me did wonder if he wouldn't go straight back to her if she asked, if she'd wanted to try again.

Emma and I went to Arduthie Primary in Stonehaven all

the way from Nursery to Primary 7. I was quite a shy child but had a good, solid group of friends throughout my junior-school years. Nonetheless, I was often in trouble, even if I'd not myself been the one to commit the crime. I have to say, I wasn't great at the whole learning thing. I found English and maths difficult and boring in equal measure, and my mind drifted in lesson time all too easily.

In addition, I found myself having quite frequent arguments with other kids. And maybe, looking back on it, I was even a bit of a bully. Obviously, I deeply regret it now. A few years back, I ran into a girl called Rachel who'd been in my class – she was clever but always seemed to be where you didn't want her. Always hanging around. I remember my best friend and I picked on her, and took her lunch. If I saw her today, I'd apologise unreservedly. She didn't deserve it, and there was no reason for it, none at all.

By the same token, I myself was picked on throughout school, too, usually for small things. I was left out from party invitations or teased about inconsequential things – too small to recall now. But I remember the atmosphere.

I was always interested in hair. In fact, four doors down lived a little girl just two years younger than me. I remember her loving Atomic Kitten – she had the CD, and on the front cover, there was a picture of the singers, one of whom had very short hair. 'I'd love to have her hair,' sighed my neighbour. And so we sat down there on the front doorstep, and I cut most of her hair off. Her mum went mad, of course, and called me 'the hairdresser' thereafter. But it was an early sign of what was to come.

Meanwhile, at home, Emma and I fought like cat and dog. We'd argue about anything: the TV remote, the half-hourly slots we were given on the computer (which lived in its own nook under the staircase) and the way I'd count down the seconds until it was my turn. I railed against any occasion when she was given the advantage over me due to her age – I wasn't having any of that, oh no. Having said that, we were close as kids, too. We had the same friends on our street and often played all together. While we might slam doors in each other's faces from time to time, we were, and remain, true sisters. It's a love/hate relationship where love usually wins out. And I think we were lucky to have each other growing up.

Emma's Wedding – Leanne, Emma (Sister), Gill (Mum)

Emma's home Henny (Emma, Leanne, Gill)

5
LEANNE PART 2

Emma and I both attended Mackie Academy for secondary school. I can distinctly remember going for a tour of our new school beforehand and walking into a huge hall – a hall for much bigger kids than I was used to. Soon I'd be leaving Primary 7 and heading into this new world of tall teenagers, hairspray and chewing gum, with cigarettes smoked in secret round the back of the gym. If you had an elder sibling, you'd automatically be placed into the same house as them, and I still recall groaning internally when I realised this. Our house colours were pure mustard yellow, and it meant that everything – from our PE socks and T-shirts – was emblazoned with this hideous colour.

On this introductory tour day of the school, we were introduced to kids from other surrounding primaries who'd be in the same year. Thankfully, I was put with Sarah, my friend from the juniors, and we were already good mates. When I met Hannah on my first day – she'd gone to a different primary – we instantly hit it off. We couldn't really have been more different: she was super sporty, for instance, while I wasn't, and she was also super smart. I didn't consider myself to be academic in the slightest. In fact, the group I hung around with most frequently in my first year of this new school were all quite smart.

As the years went by, different factors meant we saw less and less of each other – we might have chosen different subjects, for instance, or been streamed into different sets – and I slowly fell in with a less positive group. I went seemingly overnight from being a quiet, diligent sort of student to much more outspoken, spending my time with kids who drank and smoked and didn't pay attention in class. We got ourselves in all sorts of trouble; we skived off school and generally did our best not to involve ourselves with anything so dull as extracurricular activities. I think, looking back, that if I'd stayed friends with the original group, I'd have had a better education overall. Nowadays, I can see on social media that my second group are still close to one another – still very much in each other's lives.

When it came to exams, the best grade I achieved was in drama. We had to write a short act with three or four other students and perform it – my teacher said our group's was one of the best. She even said I should have gone to drama school. I suppose that in another life, if I'd pursued this, I could well have done that. I was close to being in the bottom sets for maths and English, and theatre did feel like an outlet of sorts. I found spelling, grammar and punctuation difficult, and without these, it can be quite hard to express yourself in most humanities subjects, like history and geography. In the end, for our GCSEs, I was put into a combined humanities course that didn't specialise in any one subject but was more of a broad overview.

It's a tough one, streaming kids in school. I think, on one level, it's a great idea because it means teachers can tailor lessons to the abilities of their students. Everyone gets the help and support they need, or if they're doing well, they are challenged and pushed further to achieve even more. The only problem is when you feel that your school has basically already given up on you, when everyone else in the class is a distraction and you wish you could just leave school altogether – you're not learning anything.

Not only did school seem a total waste of time, but my mum and I just seemed to be fighting all the time. We had countless conversations after parents' evenings – chats that would inevitably descend into anger on her part, exasperation on mine.

'Just stop messing around, Leanne,' she'd fume. 'All those teachers said how much potential you have, how you could be doing so much better.'

'I know,' I'd respond sulkily.

'It's not that you can't learn – it's that you're choosing not to.'

And she was right. I wanted to be a class clown, wanted to make people – as well as myself – laugh, and I truly didn't think it would impact my life as I grew older. I do notice it even today, the difficulty I have with spelling in particular, and I'm thankful that Calvin is a bit better in that department and I can check things with him when I need to.

It's a tough one, I know, because as a parent now, I can see the difficulty of balancing wanting your child to enjoy themselves at school and managing your own expectations about how they'll perform. My own dad didn't have much of an input when it came to advice or words of guidance, and I'm happy to know it'll be different for Cobi, that we'll both support him and guide him as necessary throughout his school career. Dad was a much more relaxed parent overall, I think. Mum would often ask him to deal with me when I was being difficult, as all teenagers are.

'Just sort her out please, Ray,' she'd say, exasperated. He'd smile at me and whisper, 'Shall we go for an ice cream?'

Mum was the one who'd grill me on my next steps, on exactly what I planned to do with my life after school and where I saw myself. In some ways, it was easier for Emma because she went straight through secondary school and into college, where she specialised in photography and was very successful at it. By the time I came to my fourth year, at the age of 16, I was more than ready to leave full-time education altogether.

'Fine,' said Mum, 'but if you are leaving, you need to find something to do. I'm not having you aimlessly bumming around. Got it?'

Mums, eh? Tough love. But she was right. I had no intention of leaving school to do nothing, by the way – I just wanted to be out of that environment, away from the endless back and forth of getting X grade to move onto Y topic, doing silly pieces of coursework that didn't mean anything. It was the same thing over and over, rinse and repeat. Now I was on the cusp of my adult life in the world of work, and I was determined to succeed.

I went along to an induction day at my local college and was offered a place to do hairdressing – something I'd always loved and which I could use to channel my more artistic and creative side. It was practical, client-facing, fun and interesting – I was excited about it. And then, around the same time, I applied for some apprenticeship roles, and after a whole host of different interviews, I was taken on as an apprentice in a salon. Overnight, my plans changed, and I decided to launch myself professionally as an apprentice in Aberdeen. This way, I'd get my qualifications through working.

What's fascinating to me now, as a young entrepreneur, is that it's become increasingly clear to me that I really can learn. Now that I'm a bit older, a bit wiser, I can see that school just wasn't the right environment for me. I learn things easily enough these days, through Bounty and maintaining not only that active business but our holiday-lets enterprise too. It requires all sorts of skills, from literacy and accountancy to an element of theatre in the live draws

– a bit of PR when dealing with customers, for instance. It's a whole load of different jobs all rolled into one. And through Bounty, I've realised that you can put yourself out there and achieve things with determination, especially when you go at your own pace. Not marching to someone else's tune is so important, I think. It enables you to flourish in a way you might not have been able to before, depending on the environment.

In a parallel world, I suppose I might have gone down the university route. I could have gone to college after school, particularly if I'd been good at English or maths and had passed my GCSEs in other subjects. Mum always said she could see me as a policewoman, and I think there's an element of truth to that, too. The problem is I wasn't seen as academic back then, and that self-fulfilling prophecy affected my confidence. I didn't expect to succeed in my maths GCSE, and so, in a way, I didn't. It's as simple as that, really. And I'm not sure I'd have enjoyed college. By the time I'd finished school, I'd had enough of the regimented, nine-to-five nature of school, with all its ringing bells, registration, heavy bags to haul around and the scribbling down of homework assignments. I was ready to try something else.

I was, you won't be surprised to learn, a very rebellious sort of teenager. I think being 14 was the worst year of my entire life. It was cool, I felt, to have a boyfriend. That was the first problem. At school, everyone talked about what they'd done with their own boyfriends, and there's nothing worse than feeling left out. I started dating a guy who can only be described as the biggest idiot in my school.

I thought I could keep it a secret, but Stonehaven's a small place, and soon enough, word got out. Some of my friends even told their parents – and this, I think, is how Mum found out. She went mad. I've never seen her so upset. In fact, this was the beginning of a very rocky time between us until I was about 16. She felt I'd done this to punish her, that I'd wanted to make her unhappy. Of course, it had been nothing to do with her: I thought that's just what one did. It was my decision, I told her.

I do wish I'd waited or listened to my mum's advice, mostly because it spurred me on to believe myself older than I was. I wanted to explore, to experience different things, to know as much as possible as soon as I could – a normal teenager, in other words. This first experience led me to liking slightly older men, and not long afterwards, I started dating an 18-year-old with a motorbike. Whatever we all think of such things now, it was huge fun at the time.

Prior to meeting Calvin, my most serious relationship lasted seven years. We met when I was 16. During that time when things got rocky, I moved in with some friends, being in each other's space we all ended up falling out, rumours were started and I lost my friends circle. Since I couldn't be bothered to move back in with my mum, I moved in with my ex. We had a break for a while, too, and I dated someone else for a brief period of time, It turned sour and I experienced what dating the wrong person was really like. I felt bad, but all I wanted was to find out who I actually was and what I wanted.

That time between the end of the teenage years and the early 20s are a nightmare for most people, I think. You're just flailing about trying to see what works and what doesn't. After five years, my ex and I became engaged, buying a small one-bed house together. My dad helped me with some money to put down, and I signed an agreement with my ex to state that I was 'gifting' it to him as part of our shared deposit. In addition, I oversaw the installation of a new kitchen, bathroom and garden – this last one being paid for with my own birthday money – and the purchase of more expensive things like the sofa. I loved making the house a home, in essence, and put a lot of time and effort into it.

I realised over time that the relationship wasn't working out, and though it terrified me, I knew I needed to bite the bullet. My mum was great during this time, as I'll describe later, too, and she knew that however hard it might be, I had to do what was best for me. Once I'd decided, that was it. I sent my ex a text asking him to let me know when he was home. 'We need to have a chat tonight,' I said. When we were both seated before each other, I explained that it hadn't been working for some time and that we both knew that deep down.

'You're not a bad person,' I said, 'but this isn't right. I need to go my own way. I'm not getting what I need here.'

He was so upset, and it was heartbreaking to see. On that day, he'd happened to get me a whole load of presents on his lunch break, which only made everything harder, of course.

We had finally broken up, and I realised I could both live by myself and enjoy my own company. I could be sociable with people I'd never imagined having fun with, I was out partying most nights, Life was better. There was only one small problem: my ex wouldn't sell the house and therefore couldn't (or wouldn't) pay me back what I was owed. I had no savings by this point, had paid off four years of the mortgage with him and had poured all my time and effort into that house. In the end, he gave me the £8,000 I'd put down and not a penny more.

Despite the injustice of this, we stayed on decent terms (for a short while), mostly as a result of our shared pets! I had Lola, the little dog I'd got while we were together. And we also had a cat, but once I'd found a place of my own, I'd be on the main road – not safe for a cat unused to the business of these surroundings. My ex was adamant that if I was taking Lola, the dog, I was taking Smudge, the cat, too. In the end, he backed down on that, and I moved away to start again without him. I thought that would be the end of it, but I was wrong. Shortly after meeting Calvin I received a phone call from my ex demanding I tell him what I was doing that evening. My ex had logged into my social media accounts and read my personal messages, this was quickly the end to staying civil.

If I was still there, still living that same life, I think I'd be miserable now. I was a totally different person 10 years ago, very quiet; I used to never go out drinking and smoked too much. Our lives were dull, I think. We'd go down in our car to Aberdeen Beach and speak to other people in their cars – just boring, really. And it wasn't me; I only did it because my ex did, I think. I never had my own circle of friends, I instantly found out who actually liked me when I left. Leaving the relationship helped me to find myself. Suddenly, I was going away with my girlfriends to new places, getting dressed up for a night in town, taking myself out for dinner at places beyond the usual TGI Fridays or similar chain restaurants and actually being invited to parties and social events. I was enjoying myself, living a proper early-20s sort of lifestyle. And it was around that time that Calvin came into my life.

During the early days of meeting Calvin, I had a best friend, and we were inseparable. I did everything with her, she was my rock. After the first month of dating Calvin I noticed her distancing herself. She would stop inviting me out, stop calling and eventually she stopped returning my texts. On one occasion, she even said she had to work, but then sent me a picture of herself out with friends. I often question, what did I do? After a few months, I gave up on having a small social circle. Best friends – who needs them? Calvin then not only became my boyfriend at the time, but he became my best friend. To this day, I can count on one hand who my close friends are, and who have been for years.

Leanne's days of going out drinking!

Our first weekend away (Edinburgh Christmas markets, 2017)

6
CALVIN PART 1

I was born in Dundee in 1986. Most of my family are Scottish, and it was here I spent my very earliest days. Mum had grown up on a farm and was one of five children, along with her brothers and sisters. My grandmother Maggie turned 90 recently – an amazing achievement. She's had a good life overall. I hope she'll read this and know how much she means to us all.

My mum, Meg, grew up in poverty. It was a hard life, one of hand-me-downs and money worries, and she was forced to be a real grafter as a result. Indeed, much later, she supported me when I went off the rails. Her father, my grandfather, died very young, and she still managed to make things work at a time when women were seldom breadwinners. My dad, on the other hand, was never really there for me. It was the opposite situation there: one parent was completely devoted, and the other was terrible.

It was because of Dad that we moved down to Whitehaven in Cumbria. He got a job open cast mining, so we all relocated.

And then, when I was very young, he ran off with another woman, leaving myself and my siblings alone with our poor mum. For a little while afterwards, he'd pick me up on Sundays to spend time with me, but he would often simply ask my stepbrother to take care of me and didn't seem all that bothered generally. I don't know very much about him now, apart from the fact that he's still with the woman he ran off with. Soon enough, Dad sold Mum's house behind her back despite his new partner having a good income and he himself working as a foreman in construction and earning a decent wage, too. The loss of the house left my siblings, mother and me with nothing.

There was no chance Mum would take Dad back – not after he'd cheated on her. It was a terrible betrayal and one she didn't deserve. He resented her for not forgiving him, and his new partner would often make snide comments about Mum, both to her face and to us, her kids. Now that I myself am a father, I can't in a million years imagine doing that to Cobi. Not only abandoning him but bringing someone into his life who'd badmouth my wife like his wife badmouthed Mum.

My mum is now the best sort of grandparent: hands-on, always there for Cobi, playful and fun. She's an opinionated woman, and we don't always see eye to eye, but that's normal. She'll moan if our Doberman jumps up at her – and, fair enough, he nearly knocked her down once. But I'll always make the time to go and see her, and I can't fault her for the way she raised me and my siblings.

I was OK at school, generally quite naughty in my years at St James' Primary. I can remember enjoying English more than maths, and I was quite good at PE. Mum had got a new boyfriend by the time I started secondary school – his name was Ray, and he was a good man. He encouraged me to keep my head down, to try hard at school, and his advice became a turning point for me. I began to work harder, to apply myself with more diligence. Soon enough, however, I was classed as a swot, and I realised I could continue down the goody-goody path and find myself the target of bullies, or I could change things again. I began to adopt the class-clown persona again, told teachers to f*** off and generally caused trouble. Soon enough, I ended up with the wrong crowd and became friends with the toughest kid in my year for protection.

Many years later, when I was about 20, this same person who I once trusted knocked on my ex-girlfriend's door and asked me for a lift into town. I said that was fine, but his demeanour completely changed once we got into the car, and he pulled a gun on me. I didn't, of course, know that it was a replica at the time. Terrified, I did as he asked. He kept me a hostage for some three hours, threatening to throw acid in my face, telling me he'd put me six feet under, before kicking me out and stealing the car. It took me a long time to get over that, as you'd expect. A strange and traumatic example of how school friends can become your worst nightmare later down the line, how old connections can resurface in the most awful of ways. I pressed charges, and he did end up doing six months in jail for what he'd put me through. I had to undergo counselling after that, as you'd expect.

As we'll see in the next chapter, I did try with school – I really did. If things had been different, the outcome might have changed, too. In the end, I left without any qualifications at all, just three Xs on my results letter where marks might have been for English, maths and science. My teachers thought I was a waster, and everyone had basically given up on me.

I took a job at Center Parcs by lying and claiming to be 16 on my CV. Here I was able to earn a bit of money pot-washing, and I did this for six months. I was keen to work, ready to go, but my friends at the time – plus the lack of grades – weren't working in my favour.

By the time I turned 18, I was working in construction, digging out trenches and performing various demolition jobs for a company called Lawson's. From here, I got into plaster-boarding and was soon travelling round the UK for work. My weekends were usually spent getting through that week's wages on drink and partying – but I managed to get my NVQ and bought my own tools. I knew I wanted to start my own business and loved the idea of working for myself. If things had been different, I might well have done this earlier.

Whitehaven can be a really rough place, even for a kid who's grown up with a decent family. It's so easy to get dragged into the wrong sort of thing. Everywhere I looked, there was fighting and drugs, people drinking at work and encouraging me to do the same. The odds were very much stacked against me, and I knew there was very little chance of me being successful. To be honest, there'd be Monday mornings when I was surprised even to be alive. I worked hard during the week, but at the weekends, I'd be completely pissed, high or a combination of the two.

It was only when I got into security that I really thought the time might have come to open my own business. I even had a colleague who agreed it was a great idea, that I should go for it. The entrepreneurial spirit was there, I think – I'd just never had reason to really develop it. In amongst all this, I began to think seriously about doing TV work. I'd always been quite confident, quite self-assured, and thought I could use these qualities to my advantage. Through *Coach Trip*, I was on TV for around a month in the end and had agents getting in touch – it seemed that I might be able to do more shows. Many years later, I can remember thinking Leanne and I would do well on a show like *Don't Tell the Bride* – and how right was I – but we also did *Couples Come Dine With Me*, too.

It seems funny to think of it now, but she always believed the competition business wouldn't take off. By the time the first lockdown kicked in, I was a supervisor working my way up the ladder in construction, and we had a one-year-old child to think of. I'd been working with this specific company since the age of 30, but once I got my Telehandler Operator licence, my wages went up massively. I was on course to be a manager. And then the pandemic hit.

A friend of mine, Fay, gave me a book while I was working as a bouncer. It's fair to say it totally changed my life. In 2006, a film was released that claimed to reveal the universe's great mystery – that film was called *The Secret*, and later that same year, the author, Rhonda Byrne, followed it up with a book of the same name. It became a global bestseller and has since been translated into 50 languages, selling more than 30 million copies. I really cannot recommend it highly enough, and it's fair to say it changed my life at a time when it truly needed changing. Essentially, the book is a guide, a means to use the power of positive thinking in every aspect of your life, from health to happiness, marriage, parenthood and money. Literally every single interaction you have is a means to practise what you're learning.

I read the book, and my mind was blown. I realised how much potential there was inside me, how much there had been all along, and I understood that I needed to use it. For so long, I'd believed what others had said to me – that I wouldn't succeed, that I was doomed to fail, that I'd never make anything of myself. I'd internalised all my pain and grief and just carried on like a robot. Here, suddenly, there was a tool that might prove the difference between a life spent surviving and one spent living. I truly have Fay – herself a successful business owner in Dundee, where she has her own salon – to thank for introducing me to *The Secret*. I began to ask the universe when I didn't understand. I took the time to think, to contemplate. I did the things the book recommended and focused on new goals. Suddenly, I found myself taking more pride in my appearance again, getting into shape, paying to have my teeth done, going to the gym. Soon enough, all this effort paid off, and I was crowned Mr Scotland that same year. Seeing my photograph in the newspapers confirmed to me that what I was doing, the path I was now on, was the right one for me.

I had always wanted to become involved in modelling and television work, and together with my friend Conrad, this soon became a reality. *Coach Trip* was a great experience, and we did a fair number of episodes together before being voted off. I also got down to the last 50 contestants on *Big Brother*. I was positive now and was feeling grateful for these changes in my life. I'd gone from being a dropout, homeless party animal living in bedsits to being a successful model and TV personality. And now, my life is undergoing even more of a change, as Leanne and I take Bounty from strength to strength. I'm happily married and a hands-on, present dad in a way that's the total opposite of how my own dad was. Thank God for *The Secret* and its messages of positivity. Even today, I use what that book taught me, and I will never stop being grateful for its wisdom. I'm truly a new man. All my negative influences are gone, and I probably wouldn't recognise the me of 10 years ago if I met him today.

I still struggle somewhat with imposter syndrome, I think. There are moments, especially if I can't sleep, when I worry about how and when the business will be ruined and how we'll all survive. The haters and trolls don't help. I'm constantly ready for a problem, constantly ready to defend what we've built and ensure it remains successful. I suppose this is anxiety – and no amount of positive thinking will convince me otherwise. In a way, though, a certain amount of anxiety is really useful. It keeps me on my toes mentally, and it reminds me of where I came from and how easily anyone can take 10 steps backwards. I'll never in a million years allow that for myself – that backsliding, a return to old ways – but keeping it in mind is useful for me. Having been at rock bottom was, in some ways, a good thing – I know how awful it is, and I used it as a building block, the first stone in a brand-new house constructed from all that had come before. It gives me strength every day.

Cobi's head wetting party: Dale (nephew), Calvin, Karen (sister), Kenzie (niece), Kyle (nephew), Meg (Mum) & Cobi

Family meeting baby Cobi: Uncle Alan, Meg (Mum), Granny Anderson, Kenzie (niece), Karen (sister), Calvin & Cobi

7

CALVIN PART 2

My brother, Barry, was 13 years older than me, and he was a huge part of my early life – my whole life, really. He did everything for me when I was little: he played with me, took me to nursery, helped me with everything. My life was never luxurious as a small boy, and I wasn't born with a silver spoon in my mouth by any means, but there was a definite before and after element to my childhood. The years prior to 11 were largely happy; those afterwards, much less so. The age of 11 marked a downward spiral for me that would last many, many years.

The nightmare began when Barry came down to Whitehaven. Mum and Ray were both working at Sellafield, the nuclear power plant, and we lived in a nice big house by this point. It was a beautiful summer's day when the knock came at the door. My memories of this are razor-sharp, precise in their detail. Barry came through the door very upset. We were all stunned to see him, to be honest, since he hadn't phoned ahead. It had transpired that his own dad, who worked in the fabrication industry, had sacked him, and he didn't know what to do.

Barry had so much potential. He was so nice, so good-looking. It was awful to see him looking this sad, but Mum immediately said he could move in with us, and soon enough it was thought about, with his girlfriend and my nephew Kyle, who was just a baby at the time. That baby is now 25 years old with his own baby on the way. Almost a quarter of a century has passed since the events I'm going to have to describe.

The weather must have been good for a long while that summer – and everyone was enjoying a drink. Barry, his girlfriend and my sister Karen soon announced that they'd be going into town. I think at some stage, I must have been sent to bed, and I can remember my brother coming into my room and giving me a kiss goodnight.

'You just behave yourself, Calvin,' he said. 'Look after Mum, OK?'

I dozed off to sleep, unaware that this was the last time I'd see him alive, the last time I would hear his voice.

The next morning when I came downstairs, everyone was crying. The house seemed a lot busier than normal. I had no idea what was going on, why everyone looked so devastated. I walked around downstairs in my pyjamas, calling out for Barry. No one would tell me where he was. And then there was Mum.

'Sit down,' she told me. 'There was an incident last night.'

'Where's Barry?' I asked again. She didn't say anything. And then she explained.

Barry had taken his air rifle, the one he used to shoot tin cans, and sat down in his own car, pulling the trigger for a reason unknown to any of us.

The words seemed to come to me as if through water. I couldn't understand what was being said, couldn't compute it.

Barry had shot himself through the corner of his eye. What was possibly even worse was that my mum, hearing the shot, had come outside to find her son bleeding outside. She phoned the ambulance, but the police were quick to follow, hearing that a firearm was involved. They all turned up, essentially. One emergency service after another. But they couldn't do anything for Barry as he lay bleeding from the eyes, the ears and the mouth. He was effectively brain dead from the moment the bullet entered, but this conclusion took some time to reach. In the meantime, he was sent to Newcastle Hospital, where we all went that terrible day to see him lying on a bed, all alone. The doctors explained the situation as best they could, and soon it was agreed that Barry's life-support machine would indeed be switched off. And that was the end of my brother, the beginning of the rest of my life without him.

I can honestly say with complete certainty that the incident ruined everyone's lives. It created a blot, a before and an after, an unexpected tragedy we were not prepared for and which I think we all find completely shocking, completely hideous and out of the blue to this day. My sister, who was older than him, was affected particularly badly. Suicide leaves such terrible scars, so many awful questions, a replaying of conversations trying to spot a sign. It can and will drive you mad in the aftermath. And it remains the biggest killer of young men in the UK today. A truly awful statistic, and one which I wish we – my family and I – were not a part of.

For me, I think it all took a while to sink in. It felt like I sleepwalked through the days, moving from one room to another, from one state to another, like a zombie. Nothing felt the same because nothing was. We were all of us reeling, confused and grief-stricken, but we were expected to somehow plan Barry's funeral, and deal with all the administration. There was his poor girlfriend and his son to think of, too: people who'd lost a partner and a father.

Barry was like a parent to me. I had no relationship with my biological father, who might as well just have been a sperm donor, to be honest. It was Barry who'd helped to raise me, Barry who really seemed to understand me and who'd taken me under his wing.

Only one positive thing – and a strange positive at that – came from his death. Barry had registered prior to his death to donate his organs. He saved the lives of others after he himself was gone. It was hard to get my head around the fact that his heart was beating inside the chest of someone else, but now I look back on the selflessness of the act.

One woman even got in touch to thank us for the gift of life Barry had given to her; my sister stayed in touch with her. She told us how she'd been on holiday, how she had a second chance in life. He helped five other people live happy, healthy lives. It was so amazing to think about, how he lived on through them.

I'd always been a wild child, even before his death, and had been in trouble on a fair few occasions. I was the class clown, and generally, I enjoyed it. I can remember being in serious trouble once for ripping other people's bags up with scissors. But now, following Barry's death, grief and teenage rebellion collided to form a storm of downward spirals. Now I was hanging out with the big lads near the play park after school. I smoked cigarettes with these 16- to 18-year-olds, tried my first sip of alcohol and generally made a nuisance of myself in the local area. Here I was doing all sorts of things I oughtn't to have been, but I didn't care. Who was there to stop me, anyway? Mum was at home trying desperately to hold it together. My sister was depressed. No one else seemed able to help us, and so, without any structure and no sense of future, I went totally off the rails.

Here began a truly terrible period of my life. We moved to Carlisle to start a new life. My time was soon spent fighting, partying, running away from home, smoking and drinking and soon taking party substances, too. I binged on alcohol and other things in an effort to forget. All I wanted was for the pain to stop, to feel just for a second a sense of relief, of escape. I was so angry, so full of rage: at my mum, at myself, at the world. I wished there was something I could do, but all I wanted was to make the pain stop. There didn't seem any other way than to carry on with what I was already doing.

I was about 13 living in Carlisle when I was made to take amphetamines for the first time. The lads I'd been hanging out with persuaded me the drugs would help me forget – they knew what I'd been through, and why on earth they thought this was a good course of action for a bereaved kid is beyond me. They brainwashed me, made a big impression – made me believe I was no better than them, that my days would be spent doing exactly this, being antisocial and drinking and taking party drugs. Soon enough, I'd dropped out of school without a single qualification.

The guy who gave me the amphetamines was 18, a real psycho. He manipulated me a lot and told me at the time that the substance would help me take my mind off everything. I knew that the substances they all did were bad, but I had no idea how bad, really. On this occasion, whatever it was had been wrapped in a Rizla paper, and I swallowed it whole. Forty minutes later, I knew that something was happening – I'd never felt anything like it, and suddenly, I was awake and alert in a way I'd never experienced before. It lasted for days and days on end.

I ended up in homeless shelters, with all sorts of bad

people after me. I suppose by this stage, you'd call them gangs: they were scary sorts of people, lunatics who wore balaclavas. Whenever I tried to take a step back, move out of the direct line of influence, they'd react badly. Clearly, you didn't just decide to walk away from gang life.

My mum really struggled with me during this time. For a good five years, I honestly think we hated one another, both so stuck in our own hellish worlds. We moved then, from Carlisle back to Whitehaven, and once again, I fell into the wrong way of life, leaving a trail of destruction behind me. When Mum had had enough – and fair play to her, because I was a nightmare – she tried to get social services to help me. Now I was effectively homeless, asking the police at the station if they had anything for me to eat. They let me in and allowed me to kip on the benches in the cells – just because they felt sorry for me.

By the time I was 17, I found a job at a plant nursery. Since Mum worked at the same place, we started speaking again, and she agreed that I could come and live with her once more. I knew I needed to get away from my old lifestyle, but I had no idea how. I'd finish work and go out partying, and eventually, I upped sticks altogether and moved to Holland. In the meantime, Mum moved back to Scotland to help support my gran. After a while, I moved to Wigan, got my door supervisor's licence and became a bouncer. On many occasions during this time, I made some big mistakes and could have died right then. None of the rest of the story would be written: everything would have been over before it had even started, and my mum would have lost not one boy but two.

When I was 24, I moved to Scotland, too. Now I was going to the gym and staying off the drink – determined not to fall back into my old ways. I knew by this point that I had a highly addictive personality. And I knew that if I didn't get the better of it, things would become very difficult for me. I might never come back from it. I needed to get my life in order.

It's been five years since I met Leanne. Mad to think how different my life was before, how close I came to death, how easily I might never have known the magic of marriage, of parenthood, of creating and managing a business, of being really, really happy. I have so much to be grateful to Leanne for – but without a doubt, the biggest and most important is the fact she literally saved my life. I don't think I'd be here if we hadn't met when we had.

I think there are so many what-ifs when it comes to Barry. I know that if he hadn't died, I would probably have had a much better education, maybe even gone to uni. I wouldn't have been nearly so destructive, and I almost certainly wouldn't have turned to alcohol, partying and smoking in the way that I did. He was such a positive in my life, so stable and consistent, and he'd have helped me to stay on the right path. If he hadn't died, I imagine we'd have moved to Scotland earlier, actually, and I may well have found different friends, explored different options.

Home life with Mum would have been better, too. I don't know how any parent survives the death of their child, but I know it's a process of recovery that takes many years, if it ever happens. Once Barry died, my adolescence was dominated by grief – my own and the family's. There wasn't much space for anything else. And I'd not had enough of a life before to really compare the way things were with how they became. If I'd been a few years older, I might have known myself a little better. I might have known how to spot a bad influence and understood a little more about how to manage my emotions, how to defend myself, how to cope when things get hard.

Without a doubt, I know I wouldn't have gone down the same dark path if not for Barry's death. But at the same time, I do believe that everything happens for a reason. I've done so much since his death and been to so many places – and a part of me wonders if experiencing the death of someone precious to me when I was so young might have had a part to play. I'm naturally quite open now, and I'm affectionate. I like making people happy, and I like to know I've made a difference to people, especially if their lives are hard.

I think I'll definitely tell Cobi about what happened. I'll use my life as an example, and I will be honest with him about the bad things I did. His upbringing will be very different to mine – it already is – and he's a very happy child.

However, I'm determined that he won't be handed anything on a plate: he'll need to work for his money to understand its value. I want to be the sort of dad I needed at a young age. My stepdad, for example, was one of the first people to be aggressive to me when I was younger: he asked me to do something, and I told him to fuck off. He chased me with a belt, threatening to smash my head in. I needed someone to listen to me even when my temper was flaring, even when I was being difficult, but I had no one. This will never happen to Cobi.

And I will explain to him that partying and alcohol are his choice, but they can ruin a life. I will sit down with him one day and have that chat, especially if he ever falls in with the wrong crowd. And I wouldn't be at all happy if he took drugs, but I also think that the strictness I experienced from my mum and stepdad made me retaliate somewhat. I have zero tolerance for drugs now, but everyone needs to find their own path. I was never addicted, I don't think, and I was more influenced by the people I hung out with. Even when I broke away from them, other friends were doing drugs. I couldn't escape, really. But what I really couldn't escape was a home and a family that had been shattered by losing someone so close. Time is a bit of a healer, it's true, and you find ways of coping – but you need to make sure you're coping in the best way and not in a destructive manner.

All my bad times, though – all the hard moments and

sadness, the grief and loss – they all created the person writing this today. I do think it moulded me into a person of strength. And though I wish every day that my brother, Barry, was here, I also acknowledge that the path my life took led me to another great love – Leanne, and by extension, Cobi, too. Speaking of our son, his full name is a tribute both to my brother and Leanne's dad. We take so much joy in Cobi Barry Ray Davidson every day, and I know that my brother would have loved his nephew.

Barry, Dale Calvin's nephew & Calvin as young kids with Barry's girlfriend Jill and best friend Graeme in Whitehaven

Barry, Karen and Jill

Back home in Whitehaven – the party days: Calvin out with friends

Calvin in Wigan, partying with friends

8

MEETING AND MARRIAGE

We met when one of us was about to enter his thirties and the other was in her early twenties. Here, we'll tell our own sides of the story, starting with that very first date.

Leanne

I'd been single for quite a while before meeting Calvin, and my last relationship lasted around seven years. During the final years, it clearly hadn't been working out and had become much more like a friendship. I needed to get out, and I decided to move back in with my mum and her partner. I've never been one for sleeping around, and I wanted whatever came next to be a serious relationship, one that made me happy. But I wasn't actively pursuing anyone in particular, and neither did I have a particular guy in mind.

I've never had any counselling myself, but I've always been very open and honest with my mum. After my dad passed away, the three of us – my mum, my sister and I – became a lot closer, I think, and we spoke a lot more. We started going on trips just the three of us. I was extremely close to my dad despite the fact my parents weren't together anymore. Before his death, I think I'd bottled things up, kept things from Mum – I don't know why. Perhaps I felt she wouldn't understand.

It's worth focusing here on the effect his passing had on me. Dad's death was tough for a number of reasons, not least because I was in the midst of dealing with a relationship turning sour. I was just 22, far too young to be losing a parent. Before his passing, he had been ill – having worked offshore for so long, he never really explained to Emma and I how sick he was. He'd stopped working, but I didn't know this – he'd always worked so hard. He had pulmonary fibrosis in the lungs, and I remember Emma and I speaking one day when Dad was over from Orkney, and took us for dinner. We went into the shopping centre in Aberdeen for food, and he could barely manage four steps downstairs. I told him jokingly he needed to stop smoking.

The next day, I was on a night out when my sister phoned to say Dad was in hospital in Aberdeen – he'd been coughing so much, but I thought he'd had a bad chest infection, when in fact he'd burst a blood vessel. It was too late to go in and see him that night, but we went the next day. He could barely speak, just lying there out of breath, hooked up to all these terrible tubes.

'I'm on the waiting list to get a lung transplant,' he told us. 'They're bumping me up the list . . .'

I couldn't believe how serious it had become, and yet the doctors wouldn't tell us anything – apparently it was all confidential. On the sixth day, I had a phone call from the hospital, asking Emma and I to come in for a meeting: they wanted to speak to us about Dad's treatment. When we walked into the ward, his bed wasn't there. The nurses explained he'd been moved to his own room, where we found him on morphine, unable even to go to the toilet on his own. They sat us down and the nurse explained that today our dad would pass away: they were going to turn all the machines off.

I fully expected him to be having treatment and leaving the ward, so the shock was indescribable. Dad asked the nurses to turn off the machines but said he wouldn't be dying that day, which was a Sunday. He knew he wasn't going to survive, but he wanted to have his solicitors in the following day, to change his will.

If he was to stay on the morphine, it could later be contested he hadn't been within his right mind to change the will. And so, that night, he took no pain medication that whole night – while Emma and I sat there with him. The previous will still bequeathed part of his estate to his ex-wife, and he wanted to change it. His ex had actually arrived at the hospital, wanting to see him, and we refused her entry. She just wanted money; she was a lot younger, but they were still married – just separated.

Dad changed the will and took her out of it, deciding to leave his house and cars to us, as well as a small sum to his current girlfriend. He did this, and the next day we sat with him. The oxygen was turned down slowly, and we were there the day he died.

My sister and I had to go straight into the planning of his funeral. I visited Dad in his coffin, which was unbelievably strange. I went into the funeral home with a teddy bear, to put in his coffin when he was cremated. I cracked a joke – a joke to cope – and wondered aloud if he was about to wake up suddenly. Emma and I felt bad but we couldn't stop laughing; it was the only way to cope. He looked so strange, lying there in his glasses.

After this, the funeral took place and soon enough his ex-wife asked the solicitor who the house was left to, and what she was getting based on the will. The solicitor explained she was not an executor, so wasn't entitled to any information. She went to my dad's house, in her little red car – the neighbours saw her – and all of a sudden a diamond watch had gone missing, plus other valuable items. The only person who knew where the jewellery was kept was her and us. It was such a shock. In addition, someone drained out his heating oil, which had just been paid for. You really think you've seen it all, and then you hear worse. There was nothing the police could do, really, and we then had to fight his ex, who wanted to take us to court.

She was legally still married to him, so claimed his £80,000 life insurance, and managed to get a larger percentage of his movable assets – she walked away with some £280,000. There was nothing we could do, short of divorcing her the day before he died. And when he did die, they had been separated for four whole years. His current girlfriend wasn't even in the picture, despite the fact he'd settled down with her.

It was doubly hurtful as his ex had caused a big rift between Dad and Emma, and it was only when he got sick that he wrote to my sister and they patched things up. She did the same with Dad's sister, driving a wedge between them. We had to then pay off the finance on her car, so she could keep it. She was a troll, pure and simple – a drinker, scheming and mean, just waiting under the bridge for whatever she could get.

When I was having a tough time in my previous relationship, the pressure was mounting. I felt this terrible fear that I'd be left on my own, left to fend for myself. At a younger age, while I was with my ex, I didn't live the life I wanted to and kept myself to myself within a quiet group of friends, adapting myself to fit them. It was only when Mum asked me directly what was wrong that I broke down and explained that I didn't want to be with my ex anymore. It felt terrifying, this admission. And yet, it was true. Now that I was saying the words, speaking them out loud, I did feel better. And Mum was a huge source of support for me during the break-up: the break-up that needed to happen and which led to my meeting Calvin and totally changing my life.

Anyway, soon enough I was on Tinder, but I can't say I was using it very much. It felt good to be single and free again, 23 and with everything to look forward to. Yes, I would go on dates, but I was much more interested in enjoying this new phase of my life and going out with my friends.

It was on one of these nights out that I came across Calvin's profile and decide to swipe right. I was having a good time, having a few drinks with mates, and the first thing I noticed was how hot he was. I was amazed to find, when I swiped, that he'd liked me back. It was a huge confidence boost because although I found him very attractive, I didn't think he would have necessarily felt the same way.

I did wonder, initially, if he was too old for me. But the thought was fleeting: perhaps what I really needed was someone a little bit mature, someone who knew what they were about and wasn't ashamed of who they were. I decided to send him a message: 'You're my kind of spice,' I wrote! I've never been one to have a type, but I definitely tend to go for funny, happy sorts of people, the sort who stand out in a crowd. Optimistic types. Calvin seemed exactly like this. When we first met, we were both in the same sort of situation: mixed up in the wrong crowds, partying all the time, spending all our wages on drink and going out on Thursday, Friday and Saturday nights.

We spoke to one another on the app for a good three weeks before I agreed – finally – to go on a date with Calvin. I was determined not to get into anything too fast, and he also had a topless picture on his profile that made me wonder if he was just another guy, looking to sleep with someone from the app. In the end, though, I agreed to go for a coffee with him. All this time, I wondered how many other girls he was chatting to and which number I was. I found it hard to have any trust for someone I'd never met, someone I'd simply swiped on an app, and he had a typical laddy look about him. Anyway, we agreed to meet for coffee.

My mum was always determined to know what I was doing and with whom. I showed her Calvin's profile online, and she recoiled. 'Thirty!' she shrieked. 'He's thirty!'

'He's more mature, Mum,' I said.

'Well, exactly. Has he been married?' she said. 'Has he got kids?'

It sounds bad, but I wasn't keen on dating anyone with kids. It felt like too much of an attachment to an ex, too much complication. I wanted fresh starts and no drama. I asked him outright in a message if he'd been married, if he had kids – and he said no. So he'd passed the first test before we even met. How funny, I think now, that when we met, Calvin was just about to turn 31. Since I'd set my age range preferences to between 26 and 30, had it been just a few weeks later, he wouldn't have popped up at all. Everything could be totally different.

AGAINST ALL ODDS

On the day in question, I picked Calvin up in my dad's car from the Hilton Hotel on Aberdeen's beachfront, and we went down to the Starbucks in Aberdeen. We sat down and started to chat. Immediately, it felt natural, normal, relaxed.

We had our coffee, and things seemed to be going well: we were getting along, laughing, enjoying one another's company. It was clear, I think, to both of us that we were on the same page, that we had similar values and a similar outlook on the world and that we felt the same way about things that mattered: work, family, and commitment.

When it seemed time to leave, it was already 6 p.m., and Calvin asked if I wanted to come back to his hotel for a couple of drinks. At this point, I lived half an hour away from where we met, and so I texted a friend who lived in Aberdeen to see if I could spend the night at hers, if she wouldn't mind coming to collect me from the Hilton later.

Well, it turned out not to be necessary. We had a couple of drinks together, watched a film and . . . one thing led to another, as it so often does. We ended up sleeping together. My first thought the next morning was that Calvin had surely got what he wanted and I'd never see or hear from him again. It was a shame since I liked him a lot, but when we both woke up and had breakfast, he suggested we have dinner together that very night. We planned to meet in Montrose, where he was living at the time and which was around 45 minutes from where we currently were in Aberdeen.

Excited about the date to come, I made my way back to Mum's. I felt happy, content, excited about the evening to come. Calvin had really made me laugh, and I liked the fact he clearly wanted us to see one another again so soon. And then, suddenly, just after my shower and as often happens when you're on a high, the world came crashing down. I did not feel well, not at all. In what felt like a space of seconds, I was vomiting like I'd never vomited before, my stomach was cramping, and I had broken out in a cold sweat. There was nothing like it, not before or since. I knew in an instant, once the vomiting hadn't stopped after an hour or so, that I couldn't meet Calvin that evening.

At this point, my mum was watching anxiously from the doorway. 'What did he do to you, that lad?' she cried.

'Nothing, Mum,' I gasped, and I heaved into the toilet bowl again.

'He must have spiked you!'

'It's just a bug,' I said, though it didn't feel like it.

I messaged Calvin as soon as I could sit up with my phone for a moment. 'I'm really sorry,' I typed, 'but I won't make it tonight. I've got a terrible stomach bug.'

He wrote back with one word: 'Sound.'

Clearly, it would take more than my text to convince him. He clearly thought I'd used him, that I never wanted to see him again, that I was blowing him off. I went about trying to prove to him, through many messages over the days that followed, that I was really interested. At one stage, I even considered sending him a picture of the carnage that was ensuing but decided that – after one date – it might be a bit much!

A few days later, I drove out to meet him. We went to the Picture House in Montrose for some food, and though I didn't feel brilliant, I managed to pick at a few nachos. Once again, we spent the night together, which was great. But lo and behold, Calvin then caught the bug. He sent me a voice note while he was working in Glasgow to say he'd been throwing up everywhere. I suppose it was one way of proving to him that I'd been telling the truth all along.

Soon enough, we were spending all our time together. I kept thinking he'd find me too young, that he'd think I wasn't ready for another relationship. My mum definitely felt the same – she didn't want me getting into anything too serious only to have my heart broken. But when she met Calvin, all that changed. She could see how chatty he was, how interested and how cuddly. My ex and I had never really been affectionate with each other, but Calvin couldn't have been more different, and I think Mum liked to see how keen this new young man clearly was, how he wore his heart on his sleeve.

Nowadays, with work so busy – not to mention our families, our two dogs, our son – we manage moments of stress and anxiety very well together, all things considered. I'm not one to keep quiet if something's annoyed me at work or at home, but it's very rarely directed at Calvin. The most important thing is that he and I communicate, and I speak to my Mum a lot too, as does Calvin. Having a support network outside the relationship is key, but I also feel I get so much love and support from within it.

If I had to name three of the best things about Calvin, I'd say his loveable nature is number one. He is incredibly affectionate, and in my previous relationships, I'd always found that lacking. He's kind and cuddly, and it turns out I like all that lovey-dovey stuff; I like that he's not always matter-of-fact or super rational. He also cares about his appearance, which I like. It doesn't matter if he's in tracksuits or something else – he always looks good to me. But he cares about it. And the third thing is his commitment to his family. I loved it when we went to CenterParcs altogether as a family.

When it comes to his negative points, there aren't many. He gets very tired in the evenings (but then, he's seven years older than me, so I have to assume that's the reason!). He doesn't clean the house nearly enough. And he tends to ruminate when something goes wrong. He thinks about it from every angle, ponders it, looks at it and prods it. He's a worrier, for sure, but he's also a warrior. He just gets up every time and keeps going. It's true strength.

I do think that if you're meant to be with someone, you'll find them. I knew very early on that Calvin was different: he asked me questions about myself, about my hobbies and interests, about what I did on the weekends. He seemed so keen to get to know me, in what I saw for my future and what

I felt about marriage, kids and my work. I'm so profoundly grateful that we both took that time to understand one another, and honestly, I think of all the people in the world, Calvin knows me best and vice versa. Not many people can spend 24 hours a day, seven days a week with their partner and escape without arguments – we're very lucky. But we also built strong foundations early. When we go away together, we always seem to prefer being on our own, just the two of us, rather than being with other people. We just laugh so much, and we always have each other's backs.

Calvin

I was working as a security guard when Leanne and I first met: minimum wage, long hours spent looking after an offshore building. I had so little money back then that I borrowed £20 off my mum in order to buy myself and Leanne the coffee we had on our first date. And I used my credit card to pay for a hotel room!

I always think of my life as a series of 'against all odds' moments, to be honest. We – Leanne and I – could have never seen one another again. We might never have met. It's crazy, really, how it all came together. I honestly believe that if I hadn't met Leanne when I did, I'd be dead right now. And that's no exaggeration.

I'd had four major relationships before Leanne, and one of my exes had children, whom I looked after like they were my own. I was in my mid-20s by this point, and soon enough, my best friend at the time ran off with my girlfriend. I went away to Holland for the best part of two years, followed by a stint in Benidorm spent handing out flyers and living the late-night party lifestyle. Long shifts, lots of drinking, hardly any routine. Another ex was very violent, and she actually threw punches at me. I was determined on finding a girlfriend who might be able to restore my trust in the whole concept of relationships, who could help me and look after me as much as I could her.

When I lived in Montrose, I was living a very quiet life, I needed some excitement. And so I moved closer to my best friend, Dave, who lived in Wigan, hoping for a fresh start. He watched as I got carried away, it seemed, and so despite my best efforts, I didn't feel I was making much progress on the 'new start' front.

Chasing that party lifestyle was the main order of the day at that time, the main priority. I was sucked back in, hanging out with some seriously dangerous people, and on more than one occasion, I nearly died. Once, I was almost stabbed to death on the doors of a club I was working on, but previous MMA training saved my life when I used self defence and knocked the guy out. At another house party, I was very drunk and said the wrong thing to a dangerous guy, once again, another near-death experience, a big thanks to my friend Jack for saving me.

I have so many stories from this time: some good,

some less so. A few of them are fun and crazy. Many were destructive and plain stupid. If I'd carried on more than two years in this lifestyle, I probably wouldn't be here to tell the story. I was desperate to get my life back on track.

Most of my family comes from Montrose, so I went back and focused on the gym, on my MMA training, while working on nightclub doors. People always told me I was a good guy, a great bouncer, and I felt it. But all this time, I was lonely: my life was just working out and working. I'd been back around four months when Leanne and I met, and we've not actually had a night apart since that second evening – the one after which I caught her sickness bug!

It truly was the best thing that's ever happened to me, meeting her. The bad influences attempted to regain contact. But by this stage, I'd reinvented myself, and I wouldn't have it any other way.

Of course, we all have our moments of weakness, moments when it seems all too easy to just revert back to what came before. Moments when we forget ourselves and end up much less happy as a result. While I was still working in construction, I went for after-work drinks and ended up at one lad's house. It was Leanne who came round, kicked the door down, and gave me a very firm ultimatum. 'It's me,' she said, 'or that life. What are you doing, Calvin?'

Things fell into place. I could see how quickly it was possible to transform, to forget yourself and go back to old, destructive habits. I didn't want to be sucked down into negativity anymore: surely, the time had come to put a stop to it all. It helps to know your own weaknesses and trigger points, I think, and I was definitely getting better at it. I worked out that when I was with family, I was happy – totally myself. But with the wrong crowd, I was very easily led: it was like flicking a switch.

I knew that my slightly addictive personality and hyper, often ADHD-esque character could see me jump from one thing to the next, see me make decisions I might come later to regret. And Leanne was instrumental in helping me to see that. Ultimately deciding in an instant that this wasn't the life for me.

You need to have people in your life who keep you on the right path. Nowadays, it's all about date night for Leanne and me: we work together, and yet she's still the person I want to spend my time with when I'm not working. We enjoy each other's company better than anyone else's. I find I can be sociable at work and unsociable at the weekends, sitting in quiet companionship with Leanne or chatting between ourselves, sharing moments with Cobi, taking the time to really appreciate what we have. It could all have worked out so differently.

If I had to describe Leanne's best attributes, the first would be that she's an excellent mum. Cobi really does get all the love and attention he could ever want from Leanne. She's an amazing mother, but she's also an incredible wife.

Loyal, kind, present. I never worry that she'll run off with someone else.

She's also incredibly organised, which makes up for my lack of organisation. She makes sure I have everything I need and ensures everything's in order. She plans in advance. She creates a happy, stable environment for us all to thrive in. I feel like she makes up for the areas where I'm lacking and vice versa. How lucky we are.

If I'm honest, though, I can say with complete certainty that Leanne saved my life. And that's no exaggeration.

We knew when we met that we needed to anchor one another down a little. We knew we needed to knock the drinking and late nights on the head, the partying, and extract ourselves from the leeches that wanted to continue doing that. We wanted to make our own fun, have parties that finished at normal times, remember the evening rather than get blackout drunk. It was a blessing to us both, that meeting, and we're grateful for the algorithm on Tinder that suggested us to each other! It's mad to think that one flick of a button – one half-seen, momentary swipe – could have seen one or the other of us disappear from our respective screens, never to meet in real life.

We both seemed, too, to have an idea of what we wanted our future to look like. We wanted to have kids; we wanted to be married and run a business. We wanted to be successful. For the first months of our relationship, we probably did drink too much and push it all to the extremes. But after one night out and an argument between the two of us, we realised it wasn't worth it. Enough was enough.

We both care about our business so much, and we both put more than 100 per cent into it each and every day. We're very clear that without each other, we wouldn't be anywhere near where we are today. We sit down together when something, anything, needs to be discussed. We refuse to do anything destructive, like go out all night drinking, for example, because we've both been there before and it doesn't make us happy.

When we think back to how things were before – constantly working for peanuts – we breathe a sigh of relief to be where we are. In our jobs in construction and hairdressing, we did the absolute best we could, but we lived in our overdrafts, on credit cards – everything was financed. And this created tensions, of course. We always knew we'd provide for our son over and above anything we did for ourselves, but we were exhausted. Twelve-hour days were the norm, and there was little time after we returned from work for anything except having tea and going to bed early. We made money, we paid the bills, and, if we were lucky, we grabbed a bit of family time on the weekends – if neither one of us was working.

Now we're lucky enough to spend every day together. We go out and see the winners, take their pictures, prepare for the next live draw, chat throughout the day, go to bed when we like and get up at 8 a.m. for a coffee and to plan the day ahead. When we want to take a day off, we're now our own boss, and we can do so. It's immeasurably better. But it wouldn't work if we weren't both totally committed to one another, if we weren't absolutely 100 per cent dedicated both to the job and to the relationship. We feel so very lucky that this is, and has always been, the case.

Leanne

We'd not been together long when we learned we were expecting a baby. Unfortunately, we lost that first pregnancy, but the whole episode helped us become closer and brought us to a more intimate space with each other.

Calvin had an invite to a top model event in London, which he'd been to previously, and we decided to go together. We went and stayed at the Hilton London Metropole, and Calvin booked the poshest suite, right at the top of the hotel. Calvin had said he'd a present to give in London, and although we'd talked about marriage, it wasn't really on my mind. We'd discussed engagement, of course, but I didn't think he'd actually do it. That day, I remember we'd coordinated our outfits so we were actually matching. And then we were there, in our room, alongside two of Calvin's closest friends, Adam and Conrad. The music was playing, and one of the guys – who ended up being Calvin's best man at the wedding – started filming on his phone. Calvin asked him for 'that thing I asked you to hold for me', and the next thing I knew, he was down on one knee with a little box in his hand.

We had a huge party in the room that night to celebrate. Jamie Miller from *The Voice* was singing with us at one point. At its height, there must have been between 20 and 30 people partying in the suite. Anyway, flash to the next morning, and it's just like those famous scenes in *The Hangover*, minus the tiger. The whole night was a blur. I remember walking into the living room, which was separate from the bedroom, and realising there was a funny smell. Strange. Where was it coming from? On entering the bathroom, I realised someone had been smoking in the toilet the night before. There were bottles all over the living room, bottles everywhere. And worst of all, there was a hole through the television screen, and the lamp beside it was tipped over and smashed to pieces. One of the doors leading onto the patio was broken. Truly, things couldn't have been worse.

'The place is a mess,' I called to Calvin. 'Look at the TV!'

He shook his head ruefully. 'I think that might have been me . . .' We paid to get everything fixed and left somewhat embarrassed. More to the point, that evening was memorable in more ways than one.

Not long afterwards, we noticed a pop-up ad. 'Would you like to get married on TV?' We both noticed the sign, it seemed. 'Brides and grooms needed for reality show. Apply online.'

Calvin, who'd done some 20 episodes of *Coach Trip* in the past, was confident about applying for things like this, and he knew he could put himself forward; he's always been confident, keen to add to his life's experiences. We completed the application together, answering the many questions that sought to probe us both individually and as a couple. Where did we meet? Where did we see ourselves in 10 years? We recorded the mandatory video required to enter, and then we were ready. Off went the application, and off we went to Greece.

We were on holiday, our first abroad together, in fact, when we got the call. I'd realised the day before that I felt sick whenever I had the slightest bit of alcohol, so I took a pregnancy test. Lo and behold, I was pregnant. *Don't Tell the Bride* was on the line, and they said they loved us. Apparently, we'd filled the last place. All they needed was for us to head to Glasgow, complete a second interview and sign the paperwork. When we got back, we did just that, and soon enough, we were ready. We met the producers, were told we had £12,000 for our wedding, and then we were separated. We were going to be on television – and not only that, we were going to be married on television. What was more, I was in the first trimester of my pregnancy. And as if that wasn't enough, my husband-to-be was planning the whole thing. I decided to let him take over . . .

AGAINST ALL ODDS

Calvin

We were separated for a fortnight, and it was all on me. I pitched an idea to the producers and was given the green light. From there, it was a whirlwind. Before we knew it, Leanne's phone had been taken off her – replaced with a Nokia with limited credit and containing only her mother's number, her doctor's number and the producer's. She was well and truly cut off, with her mum's Facebook feed the only distraction! She was asked to deactivate Facebook and Instagram and was effectively off-grid. I cried when we said goodbye, but I felt reassured that the next time I saw Leanne, it'd be on our wedding day.

I had the time of my life over those next two weeks. Along with my groomsmen Brett, Adam and Conrad, I planned it all topped off with a healthy dose of pub time and a stag do in Newcastle. As my mates paired off with girls, I left them to it and booked into a separate hotel once I could see which way the wind was blowing.

It wasn't intimidating, the idea of being on television – not at all. Conrad and I had both been popular on *Coach Trip*, and in fact, the other contestants had voted to keep us in. I felt confident in my looks, confident in my ability to come across pretty well.

The team filming us were great, and we got along with them as friends. I think Leanne probably found their presence more difficult, simply because she was pregnant and struggling with sickness. Sometimes, they'd announce that they'd be there, at her mum's, at 9 a.m. And in between all this, she was going to scans, getting her blood taken and all the other necessities. I knew she was concerned about the possibility of something happening, something going wrong, and her having to go through a producer to tell me. Thankfully, everything went OK, but the timing could have been better!

I know she enjoyed going along to the wedding dress fittings, trying on the different gowns and being asked to choose a favourite and a least favourite (one covered in brown flowers, since you asked). At one stage, however, the producers did come to Leanne and her mum to say I'd run out of money, mostly for transportation. It was a few hundred pounds, and Leanne handed it over without complaint – anything to ease the process.

Even today, barely six months go by without us watching our wedding video. We've been immortalised on E4 forever, and even Cobi, our son, watches it with us now. We tell him that he was there, too: he was in Mummy's belly.

What I'd pitched was what we got: a proper Scottish wedding on a pontoon at Loch Ness itself, complete with bagpipes and a life-size (if such a thing exists) model of Nessie herself. It was an amazing day – just brilliant. Everyone loved it, not least of all us. There was so much that wasn't included in the final episode, of course, because the producers have to focus on the drama, and they'll naturally throw in as much of it as possible. They'll do anything to cause a bit of last-minute stress, and in our case, this amounted to cancelling our guests' hotel rooms and the food (from a street-food van) that I'd ordered. Far from ideal when people had travelled from all over to be there with us in Inverness.

Leanne had no idea of even the wedding's rough location until the morning of the big day. She was told it was a couple of hours' drive away, and once the bridesmaids were picked up, Leanne and her Mum waited for their own transportation to arrive. And waited. And waited. It seemed to her, all of a sudden, that they weren't going to be there on time. Brett's stepfather was phoned (he went crazy at what the producers had done and said they'd also delayed him on purpose), and he hit the road to collect Leanne. I know that we needed to have things go wrong, things to spice it up – otherwise, the show would be boring. But they'd always push Leanne by asking her the same question a thousand times – 'How are you feeling, then?' – until she snapped, said that she was just *fine*, thank you: and then they'd roll the camera.

By the time Leanne and her mum finally did make it to Loch Ness, they were frazzled and tired. More to the point, they thought the travelling was over with. The wedding was to be on the banks of the Loch – that was nice. And then Leanne spotted the giant Nessie boat. 'Fuck off,' she said as she took it in. She was strapped into a life jacket – not ideal since it was likely to make marks on her white dress – and off they went.

Now one thing to bear in mind here is that Leanne was already, by this point, an hour and a half late. She was exhausted, worried and stressed. And now the cameramen were fiddling around, it seemed, trying to delay her further. 'Get in the fucking boat,' said my bride-to-be. 'We're already bloody late.'

It wasn't the safest journey. The waters of Loch Ness are notoriously chilly and choppy, so the little Nessie boat didn't stand much of a chance. They bobbed and clipped their way to the pontoon, hitting every little wave while a separate speedboat filmed the chaos from all angles. It was Joe, the main cameraman, who made all the worst stuff happen – giving signals to the boatman to turn the boat just a little and hit a cloud of spray. If Leanne had gone overboard in that dress, there's no doubt she'd have drowned: it was incredibly heavy, and Loch Ness is as deep as two Eiffel Towers placed one on top of the other.

When they finally made it to the pontoon, they heard the bagpipes. Now, I think, Leanne was finally able to see what the day was all about. I was nicely dressed, with a bit of a tan, and having arrived at last, she was cheered by everyone. It was magical seeing her arrive, even better and more emotional than we'd imagined. The ceremony was beautiful. And once we got over the drama that preceded it all, there wasn't really a better location to have made our vows to one another, nowhere so unspoilt and lovely.

We were then able to leave the pontoon and head to the

beach where the reception was planned. Of course, by this point, the producers had cancelled the food and our guests' accommodation. I know they did this for the fun of the show – for the drama element – but the food we could deal with. In the end, we ate in a large beer tent on picnic benches, having a BBQ for which everyone chucked in a fiver. The accommodation was less than ideal because it meant those who lived far away had to leave very early. Therefore, Leanne's mum, her sister and stepdad and his mother all had to head off shortly after the ceremony itself. They couldn't see our first dance or the cutting of the cake, which was a shame. I suppose in any reality TV show environment, there'll be things you shrug off and things that are less than ideal. This was the latter, for sure.

As a result, there was a bit of an atmosphere between us and the cameramen, which wasn't helped by them all sitting down with our guests after we arrived. I'll never forget Leanne's mum, in her bright pink dress, giving the producer a piece of her mind. Later, we took off our mics deliberately to avoid the team having to hear us badmouthing them . . !

We think, years down the line, that we'll probably renew our vows in a private ceremony. One with just us, our close friends, our parents and Cobi. Cyprus has always been one of our favourite places to go, so it would make sense to take a holiday there, to stand on the golden sand while the sun's shining and do it all again. We both feel that marriage is just a piece of paper, but we're glad to have done it all the same.

I never really thought I'd stop partying enough to become a family man, but here we are. Proof positive that sometimes it takes just one person to change everything, to allow things to fall into place.

I know not everyone was on board with the idea of our getting married on television. Leanne's mum thought the whole plan was crazy, not least because we'd only been together for six months. She acted as though someone had died and even wanted to arrange a meeting with us to discuss it all. I think Leanne felt that, fundamentally, she was in her 20s, and I was in my 30s. We were old enough to make up our own minds. Her mum's partner, Gary, was less keen on the idea of having cameras and excess people in the house, which was fair enough – he's quite a proper, formal sort of man. And then Leanne had to deal with Emma kicking off about it all – she was meant to get married the following year, in 2019, and didn't want Leanne to do it first. We were determined not to wait until 2020 to get married, and in hindsight, this decision couldn't have been better. We were lucky in that eventually, all our families were delighted for us, putting away any of their own reservations, and our friends were keen to support us: we felt that they had our backs 100 per cent.

I think that for Leanne, it was especially important, really. That sense of security, and also of tradition, definitely appealed to her. We both loved the idea of being a team rather than two separate people. We wanted to commit to one another. In the end, our day was perfect, with the cold waters of Loch Ness stretching out behind us. And I know she was especially touched by the rainbow roses I chose for her bouquet: flowers that have meant a lot to her since the death of her dad, since they had the exact same type of rose at the funeral.

Ultimately, *Don't Tell the Bride* also helped to boost our profile. It feels satisfying, now, to look at the comments underneath our episode and see people writing about our business, explaining how our lives have transformed since the episode was filmed. Originally there'd been all sorts of comments online – people saying our relationship wouldn't last six months.

When we were undergoing the interview process, we went for a meeting with a psychologist – mostly to see if we could cope with the pressure of trolls. What would we do, we were asked, if someone said something nasty about us online? We felt we could manage it, and when one particular commenter made a reference to her hope that Leanne and I 'wouldn't breed', Leanne wrote back. 'I'm pregnant, actually,' she said. 'And it's just a bit horrible to say something like that when you don't know anything about me.' The woman apologised immediately. It's always quite satisfying to see comments responding to any negativity today, saying that we've actually gone the distance, been happily married four years, have a child together and own a successful business. The Bounty family will always root for us, which is great – they'll defend us to the death.

Leanne's Dad Ray when he was in Monaco at the F1

Our wedding photo in Inverness (Dores beach)

Our Vows on a floating pontoon on the Lochness!

Our first photoshoot together as a couple

Leanne's Dad, Ray

9
COBI

Leanne

Becoming a parent isn't something that happens overnight. From the moment you find out you're expecting, the whole experience is one big roller coaster. And for us, it shows no sign of slowing down yet. We learn something each and every day about being parents, something big or small. There's never a dull moment. And there's so much to plan, to wonder and worry about, so much to decide.

For me, the whole experience was incredible and, at times, bizarre and strange. Proper magic is happening inside your body as each week goes by. Your precious baby begins as something no bigger than a seed, then develops to become grape-sized, tomato-sized, potato-sized. As time went on, I became bigger and bigger. By the time I'd reached my third trimester, people kept asking me if I was having twins – or even triplets!

In fact, I'd started getting a pregnancy bump early, about 12 weeks in. We were getting married, and as a result, we told everyone before I reached the three-month point. I wouldn't be able to drink at the wedding, for example, and I felt forever starving, and my appetite caused me to become bigger much more quickly. Towards the end, I actually struggled to walk, and all the doctors explained that ours would be a very big baby! In the end, thankfully, he was a fairly average size.

You hear about cravings and strange eating habits, but it's another thing entirely to experience them for yourself. Firstly, I noticed that certain previously delicious things repulsed me. Calvin's mum, who loves to cook, would put a pork loin in the fridge, for example, and I would feel absolutely sick to my stomach on seeing it. I couldn't even look at meat, in fact, and even to this day, I can't really eat pork. The associations are too strong. At night, I can remember creeping to the freezer to crunch on ice cubes, and in the morning, I'd constantly be asking Calvin to go out and get me a full-fat Coke and a cake from the counter, things I'd not normally have requested.

I wanted everything in sight, and my mum actually told me at one point that I needed to stop eating for two and 'stop shoving things in my mouth'. Mums, eh? But she was right because before I fell pregnant, I'd been a size 10, and when my bump disappeared after the birth, I was a size 16 and had never felt so big in my life.

At 38 weeks, I was told by my doctors that our baby's head was engaged. I was so uncomfortable by this point, and it seemed we were ready to go. I'd sit at home on the big bouncy ball in the living room, willing the baby to arrive. But nothing was happening, and in the end, I was invited in for a cervical sweep.

I felt this wouldn't be too bad since, throughout pregnancy, there are all sorts of checks and examinations, both internal and external. But I spent the whole procedure gripping the side of the bed, totally shocked by how awful this was. 'Is she looking for spare change up there?' I asked Calvin through my teeth. When I left the hospital afterwards, I could barely walk. Not the best of starts, really. Thankfully, the second sweep was performed by a midwife with a much gentler hand. Still, nothing.

And so I was booked in to be induced. It was a Sunday, I remember, and Calvin was outside with his mum, painting my newly erected salon-to-be. I'd been getting myself ready for the birth – taking my time in the shower, applying fake tan, doing all that self-care that's so important. I had a towel on my head and Calvin's dressing gown on, and I felt good. And then, my bump touched the side of the dressing table, and I looked down in surprise. Was I wetting myself? In a flash, I realised my waters were breaking.

I ran through the hallway as Lola, our dog, came running after me, licking the waters off the floor. I screamed out for Calvin, and I've never seen anyone turn so pale so quickly.

His mum leapt into action – she's had three kids, after all – and she told me not to worry, to take a seat, put my pyjamas on and calmly call the midwife.

'Put the timer on for us,' said the staff at the hospital, 'and begin to count your contractions.' I was so panicked by this point and honestly couldn't pinpoint what was a contraction and what was just general, all-consuming pain.

'You'll know what's a contraction and what's not, Leanne,' said my mum down the phone. 'Contractions *hurt*.'

The hospital advised me to come in, so in we went. I wasn't yet 4cm dilated, so I was on the midwives' unit with only gas and air for hours on end. The contractions came and went. Soon the doctors approached to tell me that they needed the space for other mums-to-be, people who were further along than me, and that I could either choose to be admitted to another ward or go home to wait some more. I decided to stay and then began the long wait. I couldn't sleep at all, I was in so much pain, and Calvin – who'd come from work – was totally exhausted, too. Eventually, I was taken into a labour ward, my mind completely consumed by getting this baby out, and my waters were broken again with what looked like a long knitting needle. I don't know how she managed it, but Mum sat there the entire time with a cup of coffee, right at the business end, fascinated by everything that was happening. I'm surprised she wasn't scarred; Calvin decided to remain by my head!

I was given a hormone drip next, which makes

contractions worse than 'natural' ones. Now I had morphine going into one leg while hormones entered through my hand. By this point, I was totally away with the fairies, and I felt an overwhelming urge to push, though the pain was indescribable. I'd always maintained that under no circumstances would I be having an epidural, but now here we were, and they were strongly suggesting I take that option. I waited for an hour and a half, balancing on the end of my bed, almost unable to breathe with the agony.

Eventually, a very young midwife came in and attempted to give me the epidural, asking me to please lean over the side of the bed and to stay still. Anyone who's given birth will know how hard it is to do this when your body is literally cramping violently every few minutes. She tried and tried and tried again – six times, she punctured my back with a needle before deciding to go and get someone with more experience. Though I was totally drugged up, I can remember feeling appalled at this. More experience! The epidural needles can paralyse you if they're not inserted correctly, and that was truly the last thing I needed when I was about to welcome my first child into the world.

The next nurse did manage to give me the epidural as required, but she told me it might not take effect – we might be too far gone. She had a device in her hand: clicking it released the painkillers, and I asked her to please do that – immediately.

'I think it's working,' she said as I shook my head. When

she sprayed cold air on my legs to check, I could feel it completely – and by this point, I should have been numb from the waist down.

It was 15th January 2019. A day that changed our lives forever. One moment, we were Calvin and Leanne, a couple, two people, married. The next, we were parents, a mother and a father, responsible for the rest of our lives for this little person. It's astonishing how vulnerable a baby really is, the way they can do literally nothing for themselves when they're born – not even lift their heads. It gives you this enormous, all-encompassing feeling of protectiveness, of watchfulness. I suppose parenthood really taps into that ancient part of our brain, the one that's willing to fight and die for our offspring. Suddenly, everything that came before having a child seemed insignificant. We couldn't believe how we'd worried before Cobi – every concern or fear appeared tiny now – inconsequential.

After the birth, Calvin took a picture of my back. He says it still gives him chills thinking about the epidural to this day. The needle was massive, he said, and he was absolutely panicking by this point, wondering how on earth I was going to cope with the pain and, what was worse, was I going to be OK? One wrong move and I'd be paralysed forever.

I started off with a midwife who came and took my blood before two older midwives arrived – it was they who really pushed for me to have the epidural, and then they clocked off just as I was really starting to push in earnest.

Next came two younger midwives, the ones who actually gave me the epidural. Now I had my little button to click for the morphine injections. And gas and air – which made me incredibly thirsty – were on tap by this point, too. I drank about four bottles of Lucozade Sport just because every time it seemed like my thirst had gone, there it was again.

So now here I was, pushing and pushing. I remember at one stage asking my mum if I'd gone to the loo in the bed, and she (not very convincingly) said no. But then, of course, I had the nurse asking me to lift my bottom up so she could change the sheets. It happens, I suppose, and honestly, in that moment, I didn't give a crap, pardon the pun. All I wanted now was to deliver this baby, and it required much more concentration than I expected. My whole body just wanted to push down, to give me that release.

At nine minutes past nine in the morning, finally, our boy arrived. We'd waited for this moment for so long – not just in the many months since we'd found out we were expecting but here in the hospital. He was here in the world at last. 'Welcome to the world, Cobi Davidson,' said Calvin, who was in floods of tears.

I remember holding him for those first few minutes – still totally confused and spaced out, and then the nurses asked me to come and have a shower. I was helped into a wheelchair, but when we got to the shower stall, they asked me to head on in and said they'd be back to help me to the room afterwards. When I came out, though, feeling so much better after a wash, there was no one there. I was in my nightie, high as a kite, my hair all wet, looking for my family in every room I passed. And then I heard Calvin and the nurses and my mum calling for me, and I found my way back!

Mum was amazing through the birth, I must say. She thought it was the most amazing day ever, and she had wanted to be present because she'd never seen someone giving birth before. If it was at all hard for her – to see us stressed, to see me in pain, the failed epidural attempts, the pushing, the mess – she didn't show it. I think she wanted the experience, and I was glad to have her there.

We knew we were having a boy prior to Cobi's birth. I can remember going to a private scan with Calvin where we were asked if we wanted to know the baby's sex. When the doctor told us, Calvin threw himself back in his chair, whooping with happiness. I didn't mind either way, but if we do have another child, I'd love to have a little girl. My only concern was the idea of living with two boys! Nonetheless, when we went back for a 3D scan, it was incredible to see the pictures of the baby's facial features – it was literally Calvin there in miniature, the same face, the same wide nose, the same cheekiness from the very beginning.

We had the baby's heartbeat recorded during that scan and placed into a teddy bear. Unfortunately, we think it might have been bagged up for the charity shop when we were in the process of moving from Ellon!

They used to allow people's partners to properly stay

over after a birth, but nowadays, that's not the case anymore. Calvin was able to come up to the ward to visit, but he wasn't allowed to get into bed with me, and the only seats were hard and upright – he had to go home that first night when Cobi and I were in the hospital. He didn't want to leave, but I knew he needed to rest. When he came back, he brought me a massive burrito from our favourite takeaway shop. Later, once my mum went home, Calvin's mum and his nephew Kyle came to visit.

Later that night, my first as a mother, I couldn't sleep at all. We had to make notes about the times we'd fed our babies in a little book, and when we got up to take our bottles, we had to wheel our babies behind us like they were in little carts, their cots on wheels. I can remember having a great and sudden urge to pee, and I looked over to see Cobi in his little tray next to me. I panicked and ran to the loo but couldn't go. It was strange, not to mention infuriating. I tried everything, putting the taps on, thinking about peeing with all my might, but I couldn't.

I walked back to tell the midwives, and one went to fetch a bladder scanner. It turned out my bladder was very full, but for whatever reason, I wasn't able to actually go to the loo, so I had to have a catheter put in. It was sore, but the relief afterwards was unbelievable. It was bizarre how many new things I was taking in, how much life had changed – I'd never experienced so much of what was now happening to my body.

Every two hours that night, the nurses came to check my blood pressure, ask me to do a urine sample, and generally check up on me. I don't think I really slept, to be honest. By the time Cobi and I were discharged, I was exhausted, so ready to just go home. Calvin came to pick me up in his car, a Subaru it was then, and we made it back to the flat as a new family of three. We have the sweetest picture of little Cobi in a woolly hat, all tucked up in his new blue homecoming outfit.

Calvin's mum came to stay with us for a bit. We quickly realised that first night that we had a lot to learn. We popped Cobi into his new Moses basket in his little onesie with a blanket on top of him. Within 10 minutes, as we sat up in bed, talking and eating burgers, he was crying again. What could be wrong? He seemed fine. It was 1 a.m., and Calvin was returning to work the next day. We needed to sleep.

There was a knock at the door, then, and it was Calvin's mum. 'Do you want me to have a go?'

We both felt a little foolish, not knowing how to get our child to sleep, but after all, Cobi's grandmother had had three babies of her own, and she was older and wiser than us in this department. We were both a little shell-shocked, too, I think. Suddenly, here we were, parents full of responsibilities and new pressures, and no one really teaches you what to do beforehand. We were all at sea here without a lifeboat. Calvin's mum picked Cobi up, rocked him a little and swaddled him in blankets. Within minutes, he'd stopped crying and nodded off to sleep.

'He was just cold,' she chuckled. I realised then that Cobi had been inside my belly, a nice warm environment, for the past nine months – it must have been chilly outside it. First lesson learned, then.

When we found out we were having a boy, I was keen to give him the same initials as his dad. For a while, I was dead set on the idea of naming him Cortez Davidson. In the end, we went online, scrolling through the alphabetical list of names, looking specifically at C. We liked the idea of Coby, with its alternate spelling of Kobe or Cobe. But I wanted it to be different in some way, unique, and so we settled on Cobi. Interestingly, we've seen a real resurgence in the name over the past years, in all its different spellings.

I'd love a little girl one day, someone we can name Luna or Lacey, Lily or Lila: well, anything beginning with an L. And I do hope we have another, but if it happens, it happens. I suppose with Cobi now three, it's natural that people ask us all the time, and I'd love to say that yes, it will 100 per cent happen, but we just don't know. I feel so blessed with our son, so happy, and I won't be gutted if we never fall pregnant again. We're lucky to have what we have. And having been through a miscarriage once and knowing how truly awful it is, I really wouldn't want to go through that again.

I've been using a fertility tracker very loosely, and I do feel it'd be nice if it happened this year. I can remember being pregnant with Cobi over Christmas, and that was quite tough, actually – not being able to drink and feeling so bloated all the time, quite apart from all the heavy food. At that point, I was eight and a half months pregnant, after all. There's no right or wrong time, is there, really, but given how many events Calvin and I now do and how much travel we're fitting in, it might be tricky anytime soon. Just recently, we had to travel to Kent and back to pick up a Lamborghini, and that took 12 hours all in. I'm not sure how easily I could do everything we need to for Bounty with another baby on the way. But we'll see. Never say never, after all . . .

Calvin

It's mad to think how different life might have been if we'd never started Bounty. I was gutted that the very next day, on a cold mid-January morning, I had to leave my wife and son and go to work. We simply couldn't afford to have not one but two people not working, and I needed to pay the bills somehow. I remember feeling down, a mixture of sadness and longing, and I reflected on how some people might be able to take paternity leave, might have generous time allowances when it came to the birth of children. Not in my line of work. For the first two months or so of Cobi's life, I barely saw him.

It didn't help that work was particularly tough during that time. I was reaching the end of my tether in construction and was being treated appallingly: like a slave, like a skivvy.

I kept imagining Leanne and Cobi at home, safe and warm, having a cuddle on the sofa or listening to music, Cobi having his bath, Leanne washing the clothes and preparing another bottle. I wanted so much to be there, and the only thing that made it better was ringing when I could, checking in via video calls, seeing how they were both doing. I felt like I was missing out. There's no doubt that if it weren't for Bounty, I wouldn't have the same relationship with our son as I do today – I see him all the time now and wouldn't change it for the world. But if I'd stayed doing what I was doing, it'd have been snatched weekends, stressed-out rushed evenings of bath times and bedtimes at the end of a long and exhausting day.

It was such a strange time to have a child, as well. Cobi had turned one when we started hearing murmurs about Covid, and from the age of 14 months, until he was two and a half, we were in some form of lockdown. The weeks blended into one another, and dates were stuck in our heads according to Cobi's milestones: first teeth, first word, first steps. By the time the coronavirus seemed to be fading in the public mind, we had ourselves a toddler, almost a little boy.

That first year, though: that was hard. We know having a new baby is challenging at the best of times, but what we hadn't expected was the isolation. Our mums weren't allowed to visit – no one was allowed to visit. How did single parents cope during that time? It must have been so hard. We were lucky to have one another, but we missed our friends and family. It would have been great to take Cobi to playgroup, to baby sessions locally, and enable him to meet and interact with other babies his age. As it was, Covid dominated his very earliest months, and there was no socialising whatsoever.

When we first met, Leanne was living in her central Aberdeen flat, and we lived there for two years – that's where Bounty began. When Cobi was one, just before the lockdown, we moved to Ellon to a lovely three-bedroom, semi-detached bungalow that Cobi still remembers. In fact, we celebrated his second birthday there.

We were only in Ellon for six months before we moved midway through the pandemic. He was then able to go to nursery; this was a huge relief for us since he was now meeting other kids, and it enabled us to have a break for a few hours each day. It's fascinating to think what a little country boy Cobi is now. If life had continued on its former path, we'd probably still be in the city centre. We bought the house we currently live in last summer.

That central Aberdeen flat was good for us as a first shared space, but it was tiny, and we wanted to have somewhere we owned together, as a couple. Leanne put her ex-council flat on the market, but the sale fell through once Covid hit. Once we did move to Ellon, we truly thought this was our dream home in that small and quiet community. But when we decided to move, we kept the Ellon house and put it on the market for rental through Booking.com.

And then we got chatting to our accountant . . . What we really wanted was a larger space, somewhere we could both work from and live in. 'You can do that,' he said. 'Basically buy and live in a much bigger property with land and units, and you can use a big proportion of it for your business.'

We had a friend who lived here, where we currently are, and who could see the roof of our home from his house. 'I've found the perfect house for you,' he said. 'Right there, on the corner.' It was called Gowanwell and it was in Turriff.

Intrigued, we went online, and sure enough, there it was on a road called Woodside of Delgaty. We stared at one another, not really able to believe what we were seeing. This farmhouse had six bedrooms, three bathrooms, a beautiful living space and an open-plan kitchen. What was more, its double garage had another unit attached to it which could hold 10 cars comfortably. The living room and kitchen alone were probably bigger than the entire size of our first flat.

Never in a million years did we ever hope or dream to live somewhere like this, but we decided to go for it. When dream homes come up, you need to grab them by the horns, make a decision and understand you'll never regret it. We completed the sale and started our new lives here. Now we can work comfortably from home.

It's a forever home, and that's for sure. We would never need anything else, certainly nowhere bigger – even if we had three more kids, there'd be enough room. And the area is safe enough to allow Cobi to play outside when he's older, to explore the local area and the beautiful countryside surrounding us.

When we moved in, we renovated the garage into a gym, a really decent workout space that's probably better than our local sports centre. It felt great to be able to do this, to create a tailor-made space that's designed to make us healthier and happier. We also have our good friend and coach Dale from Jax MMA Montrose come to help as our PT each week.

Leanne

We bought another house here in the village for Calvin's mum, who rents it from us. She used to live in Dundee, a good two hours away, in a council property. It felt good to offer her a place to live, a stone's throw from where we are, and to facilitate lots of contact time with us and her grandson, which he absolutely loves.

We also have three lodges available to hire as holiday lets and another not far from Turriff that we want to convert into a sort of luxury hot-tub getaway. The only way to survive and thrive as a business, we know, is to spend part of the money you're earning on new things for a different business – ensuring you can always pay yourself a wage every month. The alternative is money that just sits there gathering dust. It's also a key investment for Cobi later down the line: he could well end up living in one of these properties once he moves out. We want to be able to let him live as he wants to, and if he doesn't have to worry about accommodation, then all the better.

Looking to the future, we'd definitely consider sending him to private school. We have one in Aberdeen, which wouldn't be too difficult a commute. It still feels crazy to be considering it, given our own school careers. Between the two of us, we have hardly any qualifications, after all. But we want him to have the very best education, the greatest number of opportunities. At the moment, he's at a nursery just across the field from us, where he attends three days a week. Childcare is expensive, and honestly, we don't know how we'd have covered it prior to Bounty. It'd have been such a stretch, and I'm sure we'd have had to rely so much more on both our mums for help. Now, it's nice that they can come and be with Cobi just for the sheer pleasure of it rather than because we need loads of childcare help.

It would be good to know we're giving him the best when it comes to schooling. If he goes to a private school, the class sizes are obviously smaller, and he will have a greater variety of sports, instruments, languages and who knows what else to choose from. But if that does happen, we'll continue to make sure he remains grounded. Some of his friends live in nearby council estates while others live in houses close to us. He obviously has no concept of class, or of anything people in society use to divide themselves from other people. And we want to ensure it stays that way.

We've always known that he's quite advanced, our son – he was walking and talking before he was one. And he's not even started school yet, but already he's counting up to 10, spelling out his own name, and he even seems to know the alphabet pretty well, too. He's clever in other ways, too – cracking jokes, having a laugh. Perhaps he's got double the enthusiasm for making people laugh from us since we're both natural jokers, too. But we've been interested to see his obvious curiosity, his intellect coming through. He's probably more like Calvin was as a child, more boisterous – he's not shy in the slightest and will happily chat to anyone.

We'd love to get him into racing if we can: he loves his cars as much as we do. A proper little petrol head, he loves to rev the motors in the unit, and for his third birthday earlier this year, his cake was a giant Lamborghini! In the future, we're going to have a lot of fun taking him go-karting and racing . . .

It's hard to express just how different Cobi's life will be to ours. Neither of us grew up with much money, and we'd never imagined having the sort of life our son now enjoys. We appreciate these things we have worked hard to give him. I lived in an ex-council flat before I met Calvin and had a little bit of inheritance from my dad's passing, but I had absolutely no savings. He was working through an agency when we met, living on minimum wage in between his own mum's one-bedroom flat and travelling back and forth between Montrose and Aberdeen.

And if we were to have another baby, the first year of that child's life is going to be markedly different from not only our own early years but Cobi's too. We'll have much more unstressed time to spend with him or her, we think, and we won't be juggling the demands of being two people starting up a business alongside other work or – fingers crossed – in the middle of a pandemic. There will definitely be less worry for the second child, too. We worried about Cobi because we had to. We could barely afford a buggy in our old lives, and there was a terrible day when we'd spent our last fiver on milk. What next? We had no idea how to manage whatever was about to come next.

Luck didn't seem to be smiling on either of us: my parents had divorced, and Calvin's dad had never been much in the picture; he'd then had to cope with the terrible loss of his brother. For both of us, but especially, I think, for Calvin, our childhoods weren't always easy by any stretch. We were aware of money and the lack of it, and we knew better than to ask for things. It just wasn't possible to live the sorts of lives we saw in American TV shows, where kids always seemed to have their own rooms filled with treasure chests of costumes, toys and books.

It's extremely important to us that Cobi understands this, that he knows where his parents came from and what our lives were once like. He needs to know that things are the way they are now because of hard work. No one handed us anything – we didn't have two pennies to rub together, and now we're running two successful businesses. That wasn't easy, and it didn't happen overnight, but we did it on our own. We believed in ourselves, we supported one another and we tried as hard as we could. Our son won't remember those early days when we worried about every pound, every bill, and couldn't afford to miss a single minute of work, but we do.

In the future, we hope he'll read this book and understand what his parents' lives were like. We hope he'll never take for granted what we've been able to provide and that he enjoys his life while realising it's something we worked to give him.

It's such a joy to us, seeing him marvel at the cars in our unit or play with the dogs as we conduct the draws. He's one of the greatest Bounty stars we have, and a lot of our customers have watched him grow from a tiny baby into the child he's now become. Sometimes, we'll go live, and Cobi's absolutely wrecking the house behind us – jumping around, dancing, tooting the horns of the cars, playing with his toys or even knocking the camera over when we used to use our phones. People seem to enjoy that sense of normal family life, of a kid being a kid.

We don't see the point in hiding or pretending when it comes to our son; if he interrupts us or barges in, so be it. He's a child – why shouldn't he? Lockdown did seem to show people that it's not always possible to be perfect, to set up a background and expect it not to change. Toddlers opened doors, babies shrieked, cats walked on keyboards and sent emojis to managers. We think it adds to the charm, personally – Cobi should have his own reality TV show, really.

Things are simpler now, that's for sure. We put Cobi into a lovely nursery round here, and now that we know it well and have seen its success, we'll likely place any second or third child we have there, too. There's a nice sense of following in footsteps, where we now know things we didn't before these first years with our son.

There is nothing we wouldn't do for Cobi, but we're also very clear that time together, spent as a couple, is crucial. We both want to ensure we remain together as a married couple, as a husband and wife and not just as parents. Sometimes, we do need some time to ourselves, to take a little break from being parents. And it helps that Cobi is so close to his other relatives: Calvin's sister, my sister , both his grandmothers, his cousins.

We know that we're better parents when we're properly rested, when we've had a little time to recharge our batteries. It would be so easy to fall into the trap of having our lives absolutely revolve around Cobi, but it's not healthy. He is one of the biggest and most important parts of our lives, but we also have friends and family, a business to run, parents we want to see, two dogs to care for and holiday lets to manage. So there's always lots to do, lots of scope for being things besides parents. Next August, Cobi will be eligible to enter Primary 1, the first year of school.

It's still so strange to think back on those early months with him. We realised that he was a fast learner very early on, when from around day 10 – literally no more than two weeks after his birth – he was moving his head around, trying to see what was going on whenever he was laid on our chest. He stuck his tongue out, smiled at us and seemed to pick things up quickly. When he was six months old, we introduced him to baby porridge, and he was on jarred food before the age of one, sucking on his little Rusk biscuits in the meantime. And then he said his first word – Dada – at 10 months before moving from crawling to walking in the space of what seemed like minutes. He wandered about bumping into things and laughing like a little baby ape.

We did feel bad for him through lockdown, as one finished and – just a few months later – a second began, then a third. We did our best to make life as normal as possible for him during this time while juggling the demands of the business. We made some friends with three other women on a baby group via Facebook, and soon enough, we started meeting for coffee or lunch or to watch the kids at soft play.

In between these moments of freedom, he was, of course, stuck inside a lot of the time, and we wished he'd been able to make more friends in his first two years. But he was so embraced by members of the Bounty community, who loved seeing the family together on the lives. He became a proper little showman, making everyone fall over laughing by telling us 'you're not funny' when we make a joke. He definitely knows when he's on camera now.

And it's been great, since Covid began to recede a bit, to see Cobi making friends now. We recently came back from two weeks in our caravan in Cornwall, and Cobi spent most of his time running around with his friends. We do sometimes have to explain things to him – the older kids slightly take advantage in the arcades, for instance – and when we give him money to go and play, he does, on occasion, come back far too quickly without any left.

'There's no way a three-year-old has spent a tenner in the past few minutes,' we'll whisper to one another before asking Cobi where the cash Dad gave him has got to.

He'll point back at the arcade and say, 'My friends borrowed it!'

'Cobi,' we'll say patiently, 'It's OK to share your toys, but you don't need to give all your money away, and when you're in the arcade, the tickets you've won are your own, OK?'

It's been fascinating for both of us to see just how protective being a parent makes you. Your child is your little human, and when someone tricks them or is nasty to them, it makes you see red. We've both had situations when we've noticed some older kid being mean to Cobi, and we'll have to remind ourselves that the other child is still only that, too

– a child learning about the world.

He's a sweet boy – too sweet for his own good, in some ways! And we feel thankful that although he can have the occasional meltdown (right now, he's definitely going through the terrible threes – having never really 'done' the so-called terrible twos), he's polite, respectful to adults and bright. Of course, we spoil him; how could we not? But we try very hard to keep him grounded. It doesn't help that when he spots something he likes but doesn't have enough money or tickets for on holiday, the person at the till seems to just give him what he wants. 'Thank you!' he'll say, giving them a fist bump. We sometimes have to hide our smiles at the toys he seems to like the most: the children's washing machine being a prime example . . .

Parenthood definitely changed us. We were going to different cities all the time before, enjoying the nightlife, dancing and drinking and smoking. Finding out we were expecting helped to calm us down, that's for sure. We knocked all that on the head, and the next thing we knew, there we were, responsible for this tiny little human. There's nothing so important to us, nothing so vital as his upbringing and happiness.

Our gender reveal – it's a boy!

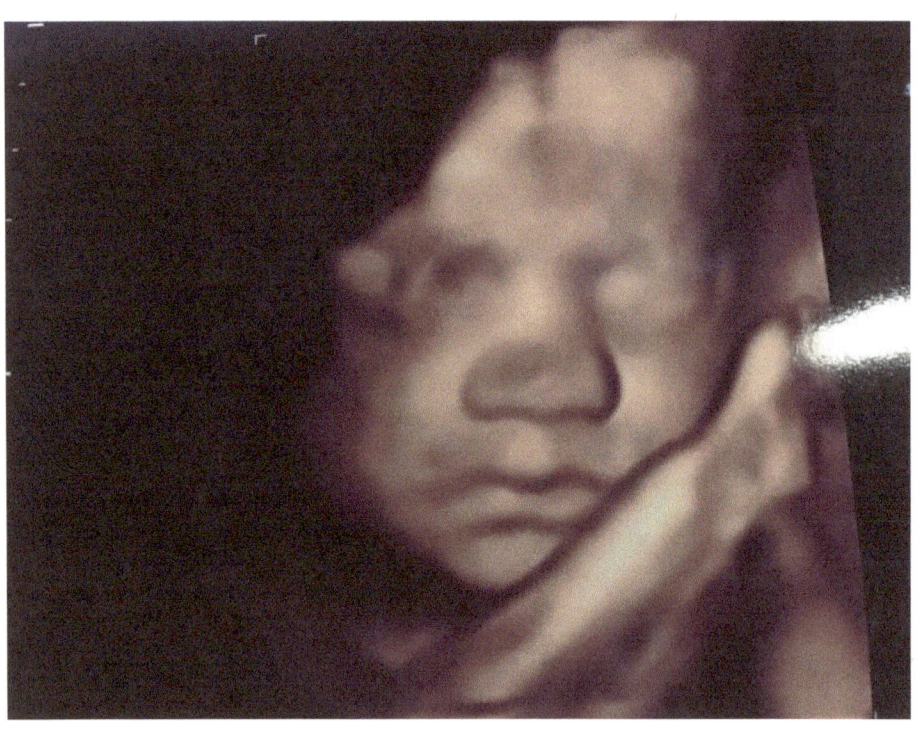

3D scan on Cobi (he definitely has his dad's nose!)

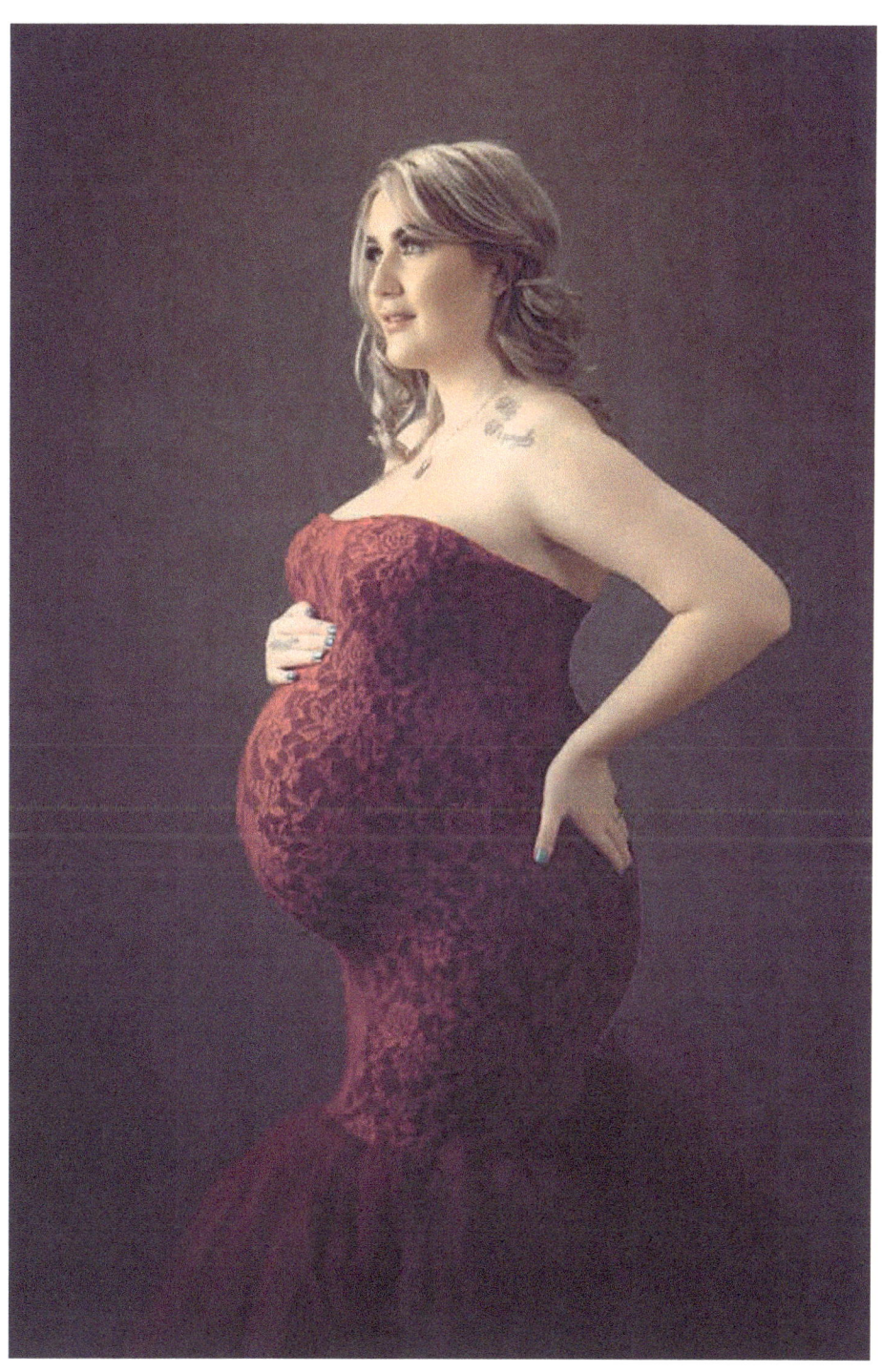

Very pregnant – you would think a beachball was up the dress!

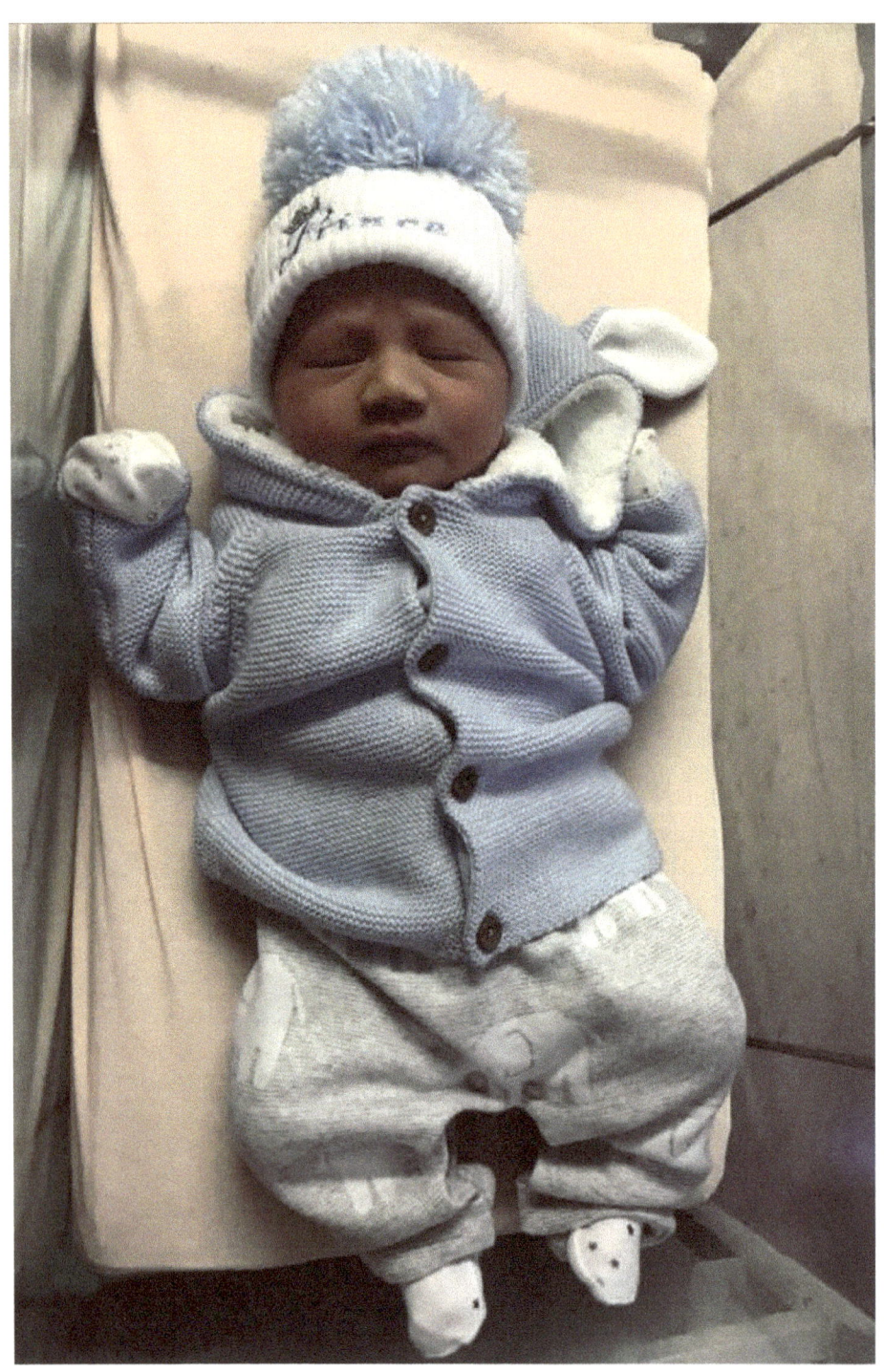

1 day old and ready to leave hospital!

Daddy & Cobi

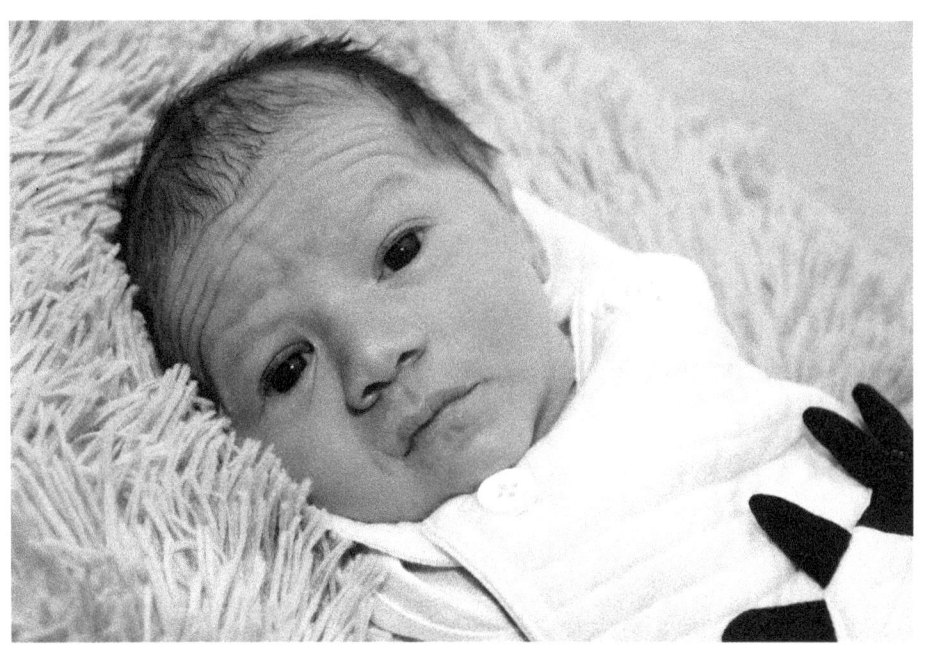

Cobi's first photoshoot at Auntie Emma's. Only 1 Week old

Cobi is one, cake smash!

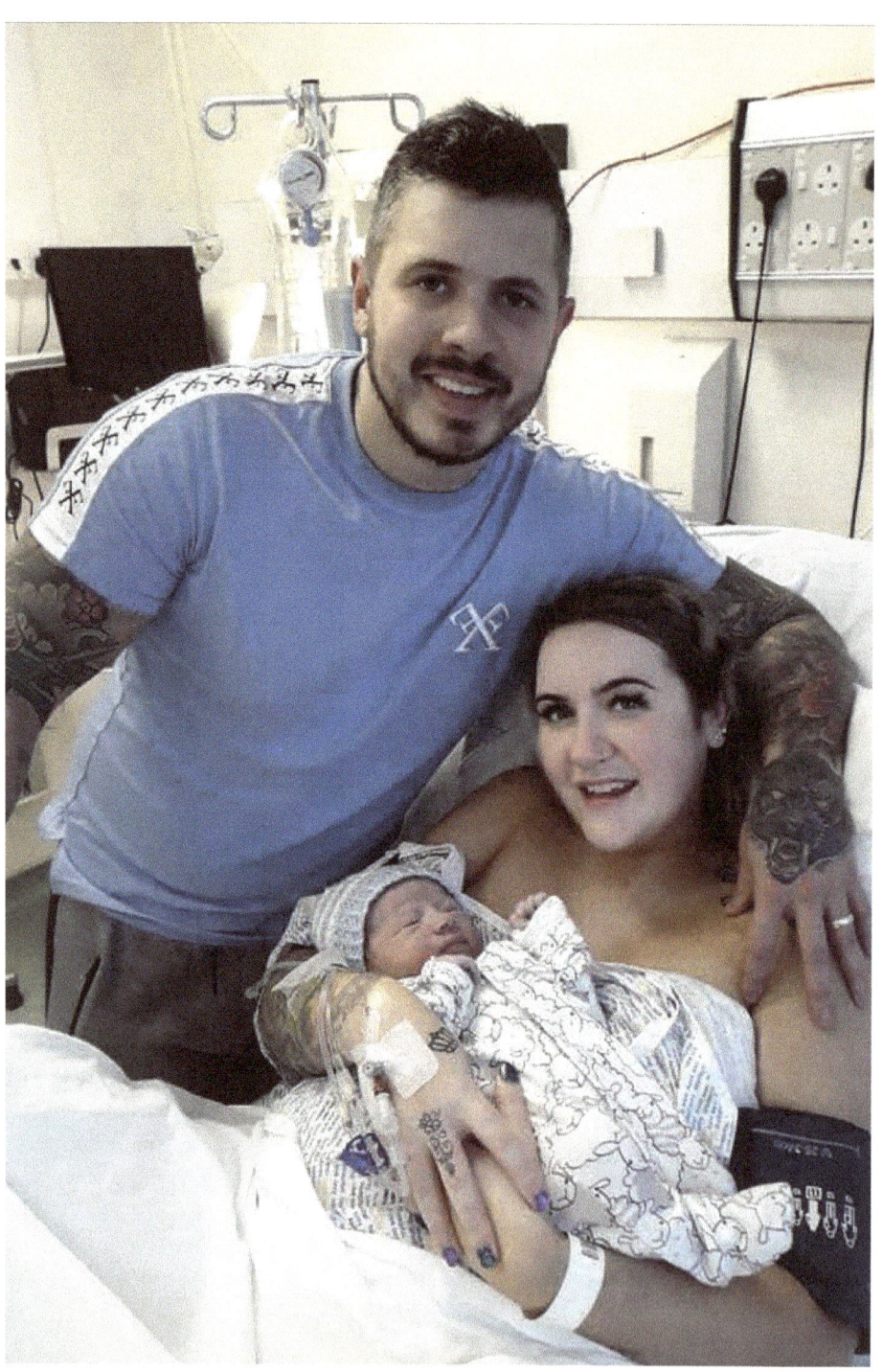

Just born, very sleepy faces. 3 long days but so worth it

2022 Pumpkin Cobi

Legoland 2022: Mario or Cobi?

Cobi making sure all the cars are cleaned for the winners!

Cobi's 3rd Birthday (he asked for a blue Lambo cake)

10
CHALLENGES

We want to be very clear: the majority of our customers are wonderful. Ninety-five per cent are a joy to work with, and there's nothing that makes us happier than seeing someone's life transformed, opportunities opening before a person who never imagined it'd be them. Money might not bring us happiness, but it can certainly change things – and often for the better. There are so many reasons to celebrate when you win a prize such as those we offer. Sometimes, they're practical and fun – a much-needed break, a wonderful luxury car – other times, they're cash prizes, and suddenly the winner sees a future they never considered possible. They might be able to help their struggling parents financially, put down a deposit on a house or flat, take their first-ever holiday or just smile at the prospect of having some savings for a rainy day at last.

When someone wins a prize, more often than not, we'll go round to drop it off – to meet the winner, shake their hand and say hello. It means a lot to us, seeing them and discussing what they might have planned, getting to know them a little, getting a glimpse of what this money might mean. We really do care about our customers and about who buys – and therefore wins – our prizes. It's been at the heart of what we do since the very beginning of Bounty.

Often we make generous donations to Charity and good causes. Over the last 2 years we have given £163,000 and that will soon increase on the 23rd July 2022 at our charity event to over £180,000.

So it makes us sad to say that there are times when we've felt like giving up. Times when it's all got to seem like too much, when the online abuse just won't stop, when it feels like we can't do anything right. We can try all we like not to look at our phones, but it's hard. Everything happens on these minicomputers, our whole lives are planned and scheduled on calendars and apps, and they are constantly begging for attention. The moment our eye is caught by one thing, one message or email, we inadvertently find ourselves spotting the negative – the comment on Facebook, the direct message on Instagram. And suddenly, it's all hands on deck as we try to put out a social media fire before it's fully taken off. Sometimes, of course, you get burnt.

There are many ways to explain what's been happening, but perhaps a story will help you get a sense of how it tends to go. We went away to the Lake District last year, just the two of us for the first night, followed by a group of family members on the second night. It's so important to ensure there's time for us as a couple: we work together, we live together, we manage our families and our son together. In every way, we're a team. Occasionally, we need a bit of time just the two of us, one on one – a time where we're something besides business partners, friends, parents. We posted a video of the hot tub at the admittedly very large villa, and soon enough, a comment popped up. How about, instead of flaunting what you've got, go and spend some time with your son?

We were so angry. As everyone knows, a comment made about one's child is about as low as another person can go – and in this case, we were being accused of neglecting him. Whoever posted that comment knew exactly what they were doing, and their words were intended to harm. Suddenly, a happy moment with your partner on a holiday break becomes tinged with sadness, becomes tainted.

If we trace it back to its root causes, ultimately, it's because we're working class and we've done well for ourselves. We know that better than anyone: we're lucky to be where we are, but we also work extremely hard. At the end of the day, people can be jealous when they spot success and become hell-bent on putting others down, tearing a strip off you and trying to make you feel bad.

One of the key ways of doing this – and the most cowardly – is their use of fake profiles. Using these, the trolls are able to get in touch even when we've deleted their original profile. We're then tasked with blocking and deleting the new, fake profile and ensuring their comments don't damage the business. It's made us nervous about sharing our lives and even more so about posting when we're away, for instance, at CenterParcs. The whole family away in one place, It's an opportunity for the trolls to pile in online and start their slinging.

Perhaps if Calvin hadn't worked in construction and Leanne hadn't been a hairdresser, people might lay off. They might look at someone else, someone with a business background, and understand how they came to be where they are. With us, however, they can't understand it, can't see how it's possible to turn one's life around seemingly overnight. They sit there watching the live announcements, seeing our smiling faces, and they get their calculator out. They see how many tickets are sold per competition and imagine that must be our profit. They have no idea about the running costs of the business and taxes, no idea how much effort goes into our day-to-day work.

So what are the worst things people have said? It's mostly related to our looks, to be honest. We get called all sorts of names and have attention drawn to our physicality all the time. We imagine the bullies – because that's what they are – just want a reaction. Sad to think they've not evolved beyond the playground. They either want to actively hurt us, or they want to wind us up, and we don't know what's worse, to be honest. Some of the abuse is likely anonymous, but a fair amount is from people we've known, even if we've not spoken for many years.

One of Calvin's ex-girlfriends, for instance, or a man Leanne chatted to years ago at work. You get to have a sense of people's communication styles, the things they say and the way they write. 'Putting money into your pockets for your lavish lifestyle,' one comment pops up. We wish they could see us at 7 a.m. on a Saturday morning, inputting an address into the sat nav that's going to take hours to reach – all so we can deliver a prize in person, on a weekend, and take the winner's picture.

We're totally devoted to the job; our house is, after all, adjoined to our business premises. We're not in the slightest bit flashy, and we're not pretentious. We are very aware that our business makes good money, but we also live and breathe it, and we work long beyond most people's standard nine to five. We've even lost friends to it, to the jealousy and envy that comes up and that some people just can't hide.

One of the worst cases we had was a malicious man who truly came out of nowhere. We'll call him John. He wrote us an email saying how sick and tired he was of competition businesses, the way they were popping up left, right and centre. And to a degree, he was right: people were stuck at home with money to spend, and they turned to fun, legitimate means of entertainment such as Bounty. We didn't think much of the email until another one arrived. 'I hate you,' it said. 'You're a pair of fucking idiots!' Later, another arrived. He claimed we weren't the type of people who ought to be running a business and using other people's personal information. It was targeted, it was rude, and it became increasingly frightening.

'This isn't the last you've heard from me,' came the next message. And he was right. He got authorities involved and even his local MP. He did everything he could to shut us down, and soon enough, he'd even started coming directly to our door while we were out. Not only was he trying to destroy our business and make us bankrupt and unemployed, but it felt like he was stalking us.

We started to make jokes about the situation – between ourselves. It was all becoming a little too much to bear, though, and since we never retaliated, we needed some kind of outlet. He became even more irate after watching us on screen, it seemed. We soon discovered he'd had his own business, this man, and it had failed and gone into liquidation. We could tell how furious he was about this, how badly it had hurt him, and we guessed that this was why he was taking it out on us.

It got to the point, in the end, where we were really scared. He was becoming increasingly erratic and delusional, paranoid, capable, it seemed, of anything. We were really scared and eventually decided to file a police report explaining that we were being harassed – both on a personal and professional level. We asked our solicitor to draft a letter telling him to cease and desist; otherwise, we'd have no option but to take the matter further. That alone cost us a couple of grand – just in legal fees.

What made us most nervous was that, in his hysteria and psychopathy, John was still writing very well – almost like a journalist. He was excellent with words and provided us with long-winded but well-written posts and emails. It was clear he was well-educated. And then the last email that arrived simply said, 'YOU DESERVE THIS.' It was all capitalised, and that scared us even more. His actions did indeed force us to implement changes: for instance, we had to introduce 'waiting to be drawn' sections with competitions posted online for at least three days. This confused customers initially, and we had to perform a live stream to apologise to everyone. Suddenly, ticket sales slumped, and as a result, the prizes became less sought-after: we were offering just one car every two weeks, in stark contrast to how things had been before.

At that point, we truly felt like giving up. What could we do? We'd go live a few times a day to explain the new system; we'd try to lift one another's spirits. We remembered all the good things we had done, and we tried to keep positive. But it was really hard, and it took all our willpower and pure strength to keep going. Only last month, John used his wife's social media account to get in touch: shocking, perhaps, but he's still at it, still looking for ways to ruin us. This is the kind of person we're up against.

When we first moved to our current house, another man won a car from Bounty, and he had it for six months before messaging us to say something had gone wrong with the engine.

'It'll cost three grand to fix,' he said. 'What you going to do about it?'

Even today, people's expectations that we will automatically be able to drop everything and either pay them, reimburse them, exchange a gift or similar – it's astonishing.

'I'm sorry,' we said, 'but it's not our responsibility to fix the engine.' We didn't mention that he'd won that car from us for all of £3 spent on a single ticket. But we gave him the number for the garage and asked him to call them. Weeks went by, and we went on holiday. Suddenly he sent a plethora of messages and said he'd contacted the Trading Standards authority. We had no problem with this, and we put it to the back of our minds, deciding to let the relevant bodies deal with something that was nowhere near our problem.

Two more months passed, and now we were moving into our new house – the one we're currently living in. Leanne got up one morning to see to Cobi and checked the phone as she stood in the kitchen. To our horror, this man had messaged at 4 a.m. 'I'm going to come to your house and kill you,' he'd written. 'My dad always told me that if someone does you wrong, bury them.' There was paragraph after paragraph of threatening messages. We phoned the police, thinking this was our only recourse. We gave our statement, and the response of the officers totally stunned us. 'We could approach him,' they said, 'and he might get 10 times worse. Or you could leave him alone, block him and ignore him, and hope he stops.' We had no idea of his intention, and we were terrified. What if he came to the front door? What if he broke in and carried out his threats? What if he hurt our toddler son?

These aren't things you imagine having to consider when you set up your average business. And sometimes it's difficult to talk about, difficult to discuss or explain. The last thing we want is to seem like we're complaining. On the contrary, the job fills us with such joy and pleasure most of the time. It's just the minority who make us feel threatened, especially the stranger whose motivations or reasons for being in touch are completely unknown. Many, we're sure, have too much time on their hands, suffer from mental health problems or are disgruntled with something else in their lives, and they elect to take it out on us. But the 4 a.m. message from someone we'd never met, telling us he was planning our deaths, was a new low. We were really frightened.

On another occasion there was a winner who won a car worth a lot, some £50,000. We should have known when he seemed so underwhelmed on the phone, that this guy was going to be a problem. We drove down to see him after the draw, on the day to see everyone outside cheering for him. Indeed, loads of our customers were there going about their daily business. The reveal was wonderful, and it was a really happy moment, with people clapping and smiling. There must have been around 200 people there, but the winner still seemed very nonplussed. We asked him to pick up the car whenever he wanted, and that's when the moaning began.

First, he said he couldn't actually drive, so he told us his cousin would come to collect the car. The vehicle should have changed his life if he'd been smart about it. He decided to sell it to another garage, and they gave him a terrible price for a quick sale, which – seeing the money flash before his eyes – he simply accepted. Right enough, that garage put it straight back on the market for £50,000 (As a garage would, as they are a business)

And then the messages began: the man claiming he'd won a £50,000 prize, that he'd take us to the authorities and all sorts. We had proof in receipts that we'd spent over the allotted amount on the car, so we left it at that. Soon enough, we were receiving messages: *I want to speak to you right now. You'd better answer my calls.* Once I blocked one number, he'd use another. His ticket had cost him £5; he'd made his own choices as to how the prize should be used, and now this. These were the times we looked at one another, threw up our hands and seriously questioned why we were doing this.

To this day, we still don't get it. Yes, they're a minority, these people. But the bad ones always stick in your mind. The human brain is like Teflon for the good stuff and Velcro for the bad, after all. We've created a family through our business, and we're very proud of it. While the vast majority are so appreciative of what we've been able to do through Bounty, the five per cent tend to hang around in your subconscious. Since we now have so many thousands of followers, that five per cent can cause more problems than we'd like.

Sometimes we do giveaways, like a holiday to Tenerife, for example, or a prize worth £2,000. On one occasion, a man came to the house with the same name as the actual winner, though he hadn't bought a ticket. We'd actually spoken to the winner on the phone and later received a Facebook message asking when the guy would be getting his prize. Odd, since we'd explained the process to him already, but fine. We told him to come and pick it up. Soon enough, a young man was standing outside the front door. He had his picture taken with Calvin and was soon the proud owner of a new Xbox.

We later discovered the original, true winner – the one who'd bought the ticket – had nothing to do with this, and he was also one prize short. *You've had your fun*, we messaged the lad. *Now bring the Xbox back, please. You've technically stolen from us.*

Come and fucking collect it yourself, he said.

We said we'd contact the police, and we did so. But once again, it wasn't clear cut. Since we'd told the young boy at one point to just keep the Xbox, the police were clear that we couldn't then ask for it back.

Look, we said. *Since you've probably taken the device out of its box, we can't resell it. But if you give it back to me, I will donate it to the children's hospital.*

No dice, it seemed. He was from a very wealthy family in Aberdeen, and it seemed like he'd been allowed to get away with all sorts. In the end, we did a Facebook live video about it which was shared across north-eastern Scotland, and this boy was branded the Xbox thief. It actually turned into something of a marketing opportunity for us in the end.

If something's genuinely broken, either very shortly after the client receives it or at the time it's handed over (and we aren't aware of it), then of course we'll replace it. But all too often, someone will get in touch with a ludicrous accusation, like the guy who called us to say the screen of his TV was broken. OK, no problem: we went to collect it and took it back along with its receipt, getting him a new one. Soon enough, it was apparently broken again. It turned out he'd hit it with a hammer because he wanted the cash alternative: that cost us four days of running around after him, unaware he just wanted to scam us.

Recently, a woman won a TV, and it was delivered by Curry's: no problems, everything seemed fine. Three weeks later, she rang us in a very bad mood. She said an electrician had come to fit a new plug in the wall specifically for the TV, that this alone had cost her £100 and that now the TV wasn't working. She'd not checked it once in the weeks she'd had it, and Curry's, by this point, weren't taking returns after a certain number of days. She needed to contact the manufacturer, who'd deal with this as a manufacturing problem, we told her.

Soon enough, her family member decided to write a post about how we drove around in our expensive car, not caring about other people or those who won prizes. Now, she wrote, the TV her family member had won was broken and she had three children at home with nothing to watch. All the sharks came out that day, and the comments were endless. *Why don't they dig deep in their pockets and buy another f***ing TV?* We were very close to just getting her a new one, but the problem was the original cost £3,500. If we bought another, we'd be seven grand down. It just wasn't a good business model when we'd done nothing wrong, and it would have felt like we were caving to the trolls.

Another important factor to mention when we're discussing the trolls is the fact that north-eastern Scotland has seen an absolute boom in the number of competition businesses cropping up since the pandemic. It seems everyone wants to run one these days, and there are at least 20 of them kicking about. It makes us even more determined to be a market leader, though - after all, competition is healthy! We've no problem with being one among a few, because it increases the standard overall. People will naturally flock to the trusted companies, the ones where they feel a real connection to the organisation behind it all.

We have two solicitors: a gaming one, who deals with the

actual website and its terms and conditions, and a separate general one for other legal advice. They're both excellent at their jobs and much needed: when we need to know who's in the right, from a legal perspective, they can tell us instantly. We've had to use them on a few occasions over the course of two years.

We had a winner recently who accepted a cash alternative instead of a house they'd won. We were, as a result, left with the house which remained empty. On our recent visit to Cornwall, we received the terrible news that there had been a huge fire right beside this house. There was an old abandoned building next door and a farmhouse next to that, where someone appeared to have set an old car alight. The building at the back of our house went up in flames, and the fire brigade were forced to douse our house in water to prevent the flames catching.

Our first thought was that we'd been targeted. It was a terrible night for us both as we sat there on holiday with our son, trying not to let our panic show. Trolling and social-media nastiness was one thing – setting a house on fire was something altogether different. We went live and tried to understand what was happening – we were a 10-hour drive away and feeling helpless. Some people shared the link to that live stream, and other haters claimed we had, once again, made it all about us.

Imagine our relief when it transpired that a bunch of local kids had started the fire. It wasn't a targeted attack, thankfully. We were so grateful, and the children's parents even got in touch to express their apologies. They knew who we were, and some had even watched our live videos. They said the kids were sorry, and that meant a lot. That incident revealed two things to us: the first being how desperately sad it was to immediately assume the attack was personal. We've been subjected to so much jealousy and mean-spirited commenting that we're justified, we know, in believing the fire to be a Bounty-related arson attack. But the incident also showed us how kind and loyal the majority of our customers are. We had so many volunteers to go and check on the house for us. While we wanted to come home, it was them – the viewers – who told us to enjoy our holiday. We had a lot of what-ifs the next day, but thankfully, we were lucky on this occasion.

It's always tough to be accused of things that simply aren't true, to be told, 'there's only one winner in our competitions, and it isn't those buying the tickets.' People will go to all sorts of lengths to intimidate, to shut down businesses, to ruin reputations. We've started a new way of managing it lately: 'pinning' now means that if someone's trolling us during our lives, we will put them on the spot and ask them to explain themselves. If they can't, we boot them out, and they're banned for life. Our block list is now running into the thousands, to be honest. But it feels good to ask outright exactly what someone's problem is – to ask them to justify themselves, because they wouldn't be able to say it to your face anyway.

In the beginning, we spoke with others who've set up competition businesses like ours down in England. One of these guys, talked rubbish non-stop and soon began to steal our ideas, claiming he was the first to think of X, Y or Z. It's so frustrating when just anyone thinks they can do it, that it's easy.

More recently, when we celebrated our two-year anniversary at the Tyson Fury match at Wembley, we were delighted to be in the hospitality section, sitting there among 94,000 spectators. It was there that we spoke with one of the biggest businesses in our industry, which gives away about 10 cars a week. One of their team, asked us for a drink and said they'd been watching what we were up to for a while; he told us to keep up the good work. It felt so satisfying to hear that someone who actually knows what they're doing, someone committed and passionate, gave us such a good review.

We want, finally, to focus on the times that make it all worthwhile. One winner's prize was a Bentley or a cash alternative; he decided on the latter. Here was a hard working guy living in a flat, trying to make ends meet for himself and his daughter. Not long after he won the money, he was able to hand in his notice at work as a painter and decorator and start up on his own. To date, we've had over 10,000 prize winners across our draws, and most have been amazing to meet, to hear back from as the months go by, to recognise in town even. They make it all worthwhile.

We don't know what will happen in the future where the trolls are concerned. Obviously, we hope they stop, and soon. But we imagine that the more success we find, the more well-known the company becomes, the more we'll have to face this sort of behaviour. The one good thing (perhaps) is that we're becoming more used to it, better able to deal with it. Our home is nothing if not secure, and we take no chance with our safety. We'll continue to take holidays and post about them on social media; we'd never give the haters the satisfaction of our silence. But the comments and thoughts of well-wishers and clients keep us going during even the most challenging times. Here is a selection of comments and stories you might enjoy – we certainly do.

> *It's because of them that there has been such a massive difference to our lives. When I bought the ticket I never thought any more about it, I had no expectations at all that I would win because we have been buying Bounty tickets for a while and have never won, so never in a million years did I expect that I would be the winner of the biggest prize they had.*
>
> *My husband Niki likes to watch the live draws when it's big prizes like supercars and houses, so he had it on his phone but I wasn't watching it. When Niki said the big one was about to be drawn I said to him, 'I hope it's someone we know that wins'.*
>
> *That night was a whirlwind, very surreal, full of family*

celebrating but I still felt like it was all a big joke on me, it was just disbelief.

When it finally sunk in that I had won such a huge amount of money the feeling was amazing. The first thing you think about is helping your family and to be able to give to our children is just amazing. Winning the money has meant we have been able to clear all the usual outgoings that we have had, it takes away worries and means that life is much more comfortable for all of us.

Seeing Niki's face when we went to collect his new car will stay with me forever. Moments like that are precious and I really feel very humbled to be in a position to do that. Things that I've 'wished' I could do can now be done, and we can have much more treats for ourselves without having to save up for them which is great. Added to all of this is the £10,000 which Bounty donated to charities of my choice. I chose two local charities that I knew would benefit hugely from the money, and there are so many others that Bounty donates to as well.

What Bounty Competitions does for normal working-class people like me is just amazing, you never think it's going to happen to you but I had as much chance as everybody else that entered and I will carry on supporting Bounty Competitions, buying tickets, as I will be eternally grateful to Calvin and Leanne.

– Sheelagh

Winning the house was a surreal experience. I remember watching as they called my name out, I had pins and needles from head to toe. It didn't seem real until they video-called me, I was convinced there would be another person with the same name as me.

I didn't sleep that night as I was inundated with well-wishing messages from friends and family. I didn't know what to do and sought advice on whether to take the cash alternative or the house. Leanne and Calvin were 100% transparent and honest about the two fantastic options I had in front of me and I cannot thank them enough for that.

Winning the house was life-changing, not just for me but for my family too. Leanne and Calvin are constantly donating to charity and they very kindly put a £10,000 charity donation in with the prize. To be able to choose where that went and knowing the impact it would make felt amazing. My partner and I chose to split it between two local charities that mean a lot to us. I made the decision to take the house and sell it on: doing so gave us the financial freedom that so many wish for. We were able to help out some family members as they really deserve it and I firmly believe they would have done the same in our position. I was able to put away money for the future for my children. I was able to make investments and make long term plans for retirement. We had our first 'proper' family holiday and made memories that will last forever.

We all recognise that things like this don't happen every day and that alongside being sensible with the money that we had to have a bit of fun too. So we are all choosing an item off our 'bucket list' to do. The biggest impact the win had on me was that with financial worries out of the way, I was able to reprioritise other issues and address them. Things that I had previously just accepted and didn't have the time or means to deal with. In being able to address these issues my own personal health and well-being has turned 180 degrees and I cannot put a price on that. My expectation when I bought the ticket was the same as everyone else, I didn't expect to win. It was a pipe dream and at £9.99 for a ticket, I saw it as a small price to pay for a little bit of hope. The odds are far better than the likes of the lottery but at 49,999 to 1 I still never expected to win. I watched the live draw not because I thought I would win, but because I wanted to see the winner's reaction. I had just went back to work for three weeks, away from my family, and I knew that seeing someone winning and jumping round their living room with their family celebrating would be a nice distraction and lift my mood – little did I know. I will forever be grateful to Leanne, Calvin and the rest of the team at Bounty for this life-changing prize.

I could literally talk for days about the changes and impact this has had and how amazing Leanne and Calvin are.

– Lee

Owning a home is everyone's dream come true . . . House competitions give someone that reality!

– Gail

Great site with lots of variety in the competitions. Total clarity on draws. Keep up the fantastic work.

– John

Absolutely awesome bunch of people. Keep up the amazing work you do! Thanks.

– Duncan

Great site, and it's local, which is a bonus. Great to know that so much money has been raised for local causes, too.

– Angie

Been lucky enough to win three times so far. First-class service by the whole Bounty team and prizes were sent out straight away. By far the best competition site around at the moment.

– Paul

You guys are amazing. I've never won, but hey, that's the luck of the draw. You put a little bit of fun and life into these dark times that are upon us. So from my family and myself, thank you.

– Michael

I have only entered a couple of times, but it is easy to enter. I haven't won anything yet, but the amount you pay to enter is quite cheap for the price you can win. The people that run it seem lovely and cheery.

– Linda

AGAINST ALL ODDS

Super easy to use app; professional service run by professional local hardworking people. No wins for myself as yet, but there is always hope. Gotta be in it to win. Big 'Hell yeah!' for Bounty Competitions.

– John

Just moved to Ellon (now Bo's Boutique Holiday Let) and reached 40K Facebook Likes – not even 6 months running

*1 Week after we reached 40K likes, We hit 50K Likes!
Even though we were going through tough times behind the scenes*

11

LESSONS LEARNED AND FINAL THOUGHTS

It isn't easy setting up a business, still less so in a pandemic. We have so many comments from people who seem to think we do this work standing on our heads. They take out a broken calculator and imagine we're raking it in, that we don't know what we're doing, that we're greedy. Our best advice for entrepreneurs about to set off on their own steam? Get used to these sorts of comments. There will always, always be people who imagine they know best, who think that they can belittle you or mock your company, try to discredit you and worse. You need to have a seriously thick skin.

We learned the tools of our trade as we went along, and we're still learning today. But first and foremost, the most important thing is to check what's in your area and see if there's an open market. Most recently, we realised that there was a huge, gaping, wide-open market where we live – there are loads of kids, but there's no soft-play centre. If we had more time, we'd definitely look into doing something about it. We hear all the time from parents that finding somewhere fun and interactive to take the kids that's also local is a real chore around here. And so, there is space for someone to come in and build what the people want. They would come, no doubt about it, and that business would be a success. You can have that idea for free!

When we set up, we knew there was a competition business in Scotland's central belt but there was nothing here in the north. In fact, it wasn't until we got successful that everyone else seemed to jump on the bandwagon around here.

Make yourselves a checklist and work through it methodically. See what's around you and what's been doing well elsewhere. Decide how realistic your goals are once you've assessed that checklist. See how big you think the business can become, and set a target that's achievable and manageable – for instance, to earn above a certain threshold, gather a certain number of likes on social media or take on a set figure of new clients.

You also need to look to the future, something most people are very bad at doing. Look at where you are and where you want to be in 10 years' time. You do not need the backing of £100,000 to begin a company, nor do you need a degree or a business-management course. You just need to research, set the wheels in motion and ascertain whether or not your idea is actually any good. Watch shows like *Dragon's Den* to see what top professional investors feel excited about putting their money behind. All of this is educational, a good tool in your toolkit, knowledge you can use. You really need to be clued up to make your business work.

Remember that where there's a will, there's a way. There will be times you want to throw the towel in, to give up and have a rest, to stop entirely. Keep going, even if the step count for that particular day is only 10 steps forward and five back.

When we moved into our current home, we had a good 30 different girls messaging to ask if they could drop off some of their products for us to try. The view was to eventually use them as prizes on the site. The only problem was that we saw 30 businesses, all different, but all selling the same product. Everything about these products was the same – they looked identical. Essentially, they had looked at their neighbour and assumed that if they set up a business, why not them? There's everything to admire in that confidence, and it's important to have it, for sure, but you need to ensure that your product stands out in a crowded market. You need to make yourself visible, individual, original. And you'll make a million mistakes before you find the thing you're good at.

As a case in point, we learned early on that marketing can pay, but you have to do it wisely. We were keen to put out branded T-shirts, so at one of our car shows, we gave away some 200 of them at a total cost of £3,000 to ourselves. The next time we did a similar show, we charged the cost price of £15, and only a handful of customers purchased. In the end, we were forced to give them away for free. Yes, it was a good advertisement for us, having some 1,000 people walking around with our brand name on their chests. It sells us and will continue to do so. But the problem was – and we discovered this that day – that unless you were a diehard Bounty fan, you were unlikely to spend money on a branded T-shirt.

Leanne

It's also very important to diversify. If one business succeeds, then make sure you're ready to invest elsewhere, to grow your pot and make sure you're not putting all your eggs in one basket. We have Bounty, of course, but we've also invested in property over recent years, and we're busy renovating another house. Eventually, we'll probably turn our hands to something else, in addition, with the long-term aim of saving up enough to expand Bounty and the holiday lets.

There's Cobi's Cabin, the biggest of our lets at Grannies Heilan' Hame Holiday Park in Embo – it has wrap-around decking and patio furniture, and it sleeps up to eight people across three bedrooms and two bathrooms. It's an ideal place for a large group to kick back and unwind and is just a short walk to on-site amenities, including an indoor pool, play park, arcade, bar and restaurant, crazy golf and much more.

AGAINST ALL ODDS

Lola's Lodge, a luxury static caravan, is found at Silver Sands in Lossiemouth, and this is a cosy two-bedroom, two-bathroom space that sleeps up to six. It's also within walking distance to everything you'd want, including the beach, and there's a great view across to the local lighthouse from the decking outside.

We then have Delgatie Lodge at the Royal Arch Riverside Park near Mains of Thornton. The whole area is perfect for an outdoorsy sort of life, and guests often head here for the paddle boarding, biking, fishing, walking and even axe throwing offered nearby, at Fettercairn. Edzell Woods is only 15 minutes by car, or the River Esk offers walks for miles along the beautiful banks. There's also Catterline Bay, ready for exploration with its picturesque views. Anyone after the beach can also find Montrose not far away with its lovely sandy dunes, or Brechin Castle's there for the culture vultures.

Our most recent renovation has been Bo's Boutique, our old three-bed bungalow in Ellon that we've completely kitted out as a smart villa. It's now our hottest property and is booked pretty much all year round; it comes complete with mood lighting, a hot tub and a garden bar. We've also just recently purchased an old-fashioned cottage just 10 minutes from home with the aim of renovation. The original cottage features remain, but we turned its creamy exterior colour to a more modern grey, converted the attic into a double bedroom and installed not only a games room but a sauna, too. It should be complete in around two months' time. We have also just purchased a house in Whitehaven which is ready to use as a holiday let once we put a hot tub in the back garden.

So does education matter? Neither of us did very well at school, and yet, here we are. If you have the talent, go for it. At the end of the day, it's only you who can make something happen, only you who knows what your strengths are and how they can be harnessed. No one else is going to do it for you.

You need to keep a positive mindset, even when times are tough – and they will be tough from time to time. Don't forget our origin story, when the world was gripped by a virus and no one was allowed to meet. Childcare was banned, all work was banned, and we were stuck indoors for months while trying to keep our heads above water. We could have lain in bed all day, depressed and broke and anxious. We decided not to do that, to take the bull by the horns. It really is all about having a positive mental attitude. If you want to make something happen, you need to put the work in; you need to try your absolute hardest and accept that things can and will go wrong. You need to prepare yourself for the rough times, for the difficulties that will come up.

We completely reinvented ourselves – and not just once, when Bounty was born. We actively changed and transformed several times over. When I left school, I really wondered what my next step might be, and then I realised I needed to use the skills I had to create a career for myself. I could have done anything at that stage and taken the wrong path completely, but at the age of 16, I decided what needed to happen next. And when Calvin chose to do modelling work, he got his old tattoos covered over, he started going to the gym, and he became absolutely ripped! He went and got his teeth sorted, got them whitened, and transformed the way he looked – eventually becoming Mr Scotland. When you really want something, we both know there's only one person who can make it happen, and that's you.

There's also the fact that a lot of people go to college and then to university, but they don't use the skills, qualifications or degree they studied so hard for later in life. Sometimes, people spend literally thousands on this further education, then leave and go off to do something they could have done years before – without college. We're not saying for a moment that education isn't important. It's crucial in so many ways. But there are different ways to be educated, different styles of learning and different criteria by which to measure success. Too often, people leave higher education wondering why on earth they bothered. They might have spent five years studying law or French or history and then leave to become a chef, a travelling salesman, a photographer or a million things besides.

We'd also advise making your business a collective one – ensuring that family and friends are involved as much as possible and that they know what you're about, how you're doing and what's coming up next for you. Not only will this provide support when times are tough, but it'll also enable you to call on them when you need help. Friends and family, or just fans of your business, can be invaluable sources of support when things are tricky. Don't forget that a problem shared is a problem halved: if you don't have the skills required in one particular area, you can bet someone else does, and if you ask nicely, they're often more than happy to help.

Calvin

I can so distinctly remember my manager shouting at me – I was on the construction site, shovelling stones, and I felt so miserable, so low. This was during the first lockdown when a few of us were called back up to work. Bounty hadn't yet taken off, and we needed the money, so here I was.

'Get a move on!' my manager roared. My back was aching, I was knackered, we had a young baby at home, and I wished I could be there with him instead of here. I needed to get out. On my next break, I rang Leanne, and her advice was simple and calm. 'Come home.'

It was terrifying, but I did just that. 'You can shove your job up your arse,' I called on my way out, and that was that.

'You're making a huge mistake,' said my manager to my retreating back. 'You'll never work for this company again.' But I had no intention of doing so. I refused to continue doing something that made me so angry, and gave me such a sense of futility and sadness.

We were both doing lives during our lunch breaks back then. I was there on-site doing them in my High Vis and speaking to followers in snatched minutes in between different jobs. We knew then that Bounty had potential, but we had no idea how much. We sometimes look back at those old videos and our very formal style, and we notice that our approach seems more uptight, even unnatural, when compared with the relaxed style we have now. Over time, we learned to unwind and to banter with each other.

I never looked back. At that moment, I realised something. My ambitions, goals and dreams were all there, and I was building something to make them come true. I could have continued at the site that day, but by walking out like I did, I was showing myself that bravery would pay off. If I wasn't going to be paid for the work I did on-site, I would need to ensure that Bounty succeeded. We couldn't afford for it to fail. And when your back's up against it like that, you won't fail because it stops being an option.

You can keep up the original work you were doing while you build your business – whatever that work might be. Just remember that if you're at Tesco or Asda, working round the clock for minimum wage, you're fundamentally making someone else rich. Those big bosses probably won't have done a day's work in the same way you have – and they purposefully put the thought of their workers from their minds. It wouldn't be nice to imagine how badly treated some employees might be, how they rush from one job to another, sleeping two or three hours a night just to make it to the next shift on time. Once you have an idea, stay positive and realise that you're now working for yourself – you're working round the clock for you and not for anyone else.

Quite recently, I went into hospital when I'd got gout in my toe. I was sitting there waiting to be seen, and there, also in the waiting room, was my old manager. He spotted me in my work hoodie and Bounty cap and smiled at me. It seemed he'd accidentally cut the top of his finger off. As we both waited, he turned to me and said, 'Well done, Calvin.' I grinned back. 'Hats off to you – that business of yours really did work out! You deserve the success.' I thought that was big of him, to be honest. It made that particular incident, when I'd walked off the site for the last time, seem completely worth it.

Another important factor is other people's reactions. Our mums had wildly different reactions to the idea of Bounty – Leanne's was more nervous, wondering aloud whether it'd ever work, while mine was on board from the start. You need to accept that this is normal. There's nothing safe and secure in the early days of launching a business – so many start-ups do fail, and that is completely normal. But you'll have missed a month's wages from the safe, shift-patterned work you did before, and that will frighten parents who want the best for their kids.

Wouldn't it be easier, they might ask, *to just stay in Asda, to remain on the construction site? I know the pay's rubbish and they treat you terribly, but at the end of the day . . . it's money, isn't it?* They're right, to a degree. That sort of work is dependable, and you know what you're getting at the end of the day. You might need to do some explaining when parents sit you down, when they tell you this won't work and you should rethink it.

In addition to keeping family and friends in the loop, it's also important to make sure that if you can, you give back. We're so thankful to be able to employ some of our family, ensuring that they not only have an interest in what we're doing but that they're actively involved. At present, we have my sister Karen working for us; she takes the bookings, usually, and sorts out all the holiday lets, while Dale, my nephew, and Brett Walker, who was the best man at my wedding, do a lot of the deliveries and customer-service enquiries. Brett's a good face for the company, and he even takes Cobi to nursery and meets up with customers and the like. Having him here as a personal assistant has been brilliant.

At the moment, we're planning to attend a big car show this week, so all the Cumbrian side of the family – who usually work from home – are here staying with us at the house. It's a full-family home, and it's great, too, for Cobi, who gets to see much more of both sides of the family than he might otherwise.

AGAINST ALL ODDS

Emma has recently left the company, coming to us from a comfortable job beforehand, working in oil and gas organising offshore recruitment. She's since moved on, but she mainly put the competitions on the sites and organised how it all works from the drawing perspective. It felt so good to not only have set up a business for us but for it to have done well enough that we can employ others. If you have good people around you, then positive things happen.

There's an amazing sense of achievement in employing our family. We're paying them excellent wages, and for us to be able to provide that for them is wonderful, especially at times like this. Working for a competition business is a rare thing, too – it's hard to directly compare wages, but we want our staff to have a good life, so we pay them extra. Karen always says that we've changed her life. That's what we're all about, fundamentally. And it helps everyone stay on the same page: it's in everyone's interest to keep making Bounty a success. We're all enthralled by this idea that started off in my head: it truly is our second child.

Andy Jones, my old supervisor, might not always have seen eye to eye with me. But just last week, he came by for a meeting at the house. He wants to go it alone as a general handyman, to work for himself and try to make a success of his own business. He wanted a bit of advice, wanted to know the best route into this arena, and he was very gracious, telling us that this plan was inspired by Bounty. He was working too many hours before, and he told us he barely had enough for a £30 takeaway each month after he'd paid his bills. But already, he's doing amazing, and I thought it was very big of him to come and check in and ask for advice, especially when he once managed me at work. He was always there for me and in return we will be there for him.

Remember, too, that people might suggest you just 'got lucky', that you started your company at the right place and at the right time. But fundamentally, we couldn't open a bakery since we're rubbish bakers. The idea that we could somehow succeed out of pure luck is insulting, and we'd suggest that anyone thinking of starting their own business should really bear that in mind. You have to do your research, learn how to market, be confident and accept that others will try to replicate what you're doing and move past that. Find what you are good at, and then pursue it. It won't happen overnight, and you need to accept that for every good idea you have, for every success, you'll have a few bad ideas and a few failures, too. And that's OK. Trial and error is where some of the best ideas come from.

We're now in a position to start offering holidays – such as the one we've just taken, to the Maldives, where we spent five days. Our own journey, in business class, was something else completely – neither of us had ever flown like this. We even managed to do our lives while abroad, something that enabled people to see us doing the thing we were actually putting up for grabs. We sold tickets at £4.99 for the chance to win a holiday just like ours. The possibility of offering this to customers is in itself enormous: we never thought we'd be in this position, that we would be able to offer holidays like this and travel there to promote it. We worked hard for it, but it still felt surreal. And now we can offer it to others.

We had no idea before Bounty that our skills lay in selling, in promotion and in the live draws we do three times a week. We're good on camera, we have good people skills and we're not arrogant or difficult to work with. These individual skills were being used in small ways prior to Bounty, but now we're utilising them to their best advantage every day. We've been told we're relatable and funny, which seems to appeal to our customers; they like that this is a family business, that we interact with one another, that they've seen Cobi grow up and that we come online and explain when something's gone wrong or when we've made a mistake. Hold your hands up, be honest, and make sure you're being human at all times.

Finally, we'd say to make sure you care. You have to care about your customers, about what you're doing and about your own brand and self-image. You have to take pride in your reputation. And you need to try to support others who are on their own journey. Recently, a girl in Aberdeen has been in touch about her clothing brand. She sends dresses for free and asks us to take pictures and post them to our social media. She's a grafter, and she's determined to get her business name out there. For that, we're always willing to help.

Two years have passed since Bounty was born. April 23rd will forever be the day that marked the beginning of the rest of our lives, the day that we decided to stop working for other people and start working for ourselves. We've transformed our own lives, of course, but we've also transformed countless others, not least for our family and Cobi.

Most importantly, we're a team. We wouldn't be here without each other, and we'll always be forever grateful for what each of us brings to this business through our dedication and hard work, the time we take, the care and graft. We want to continue working as we are, expanding all the time and offering bigger and better prizes, but we also want to ensure we take good breaks, that we don't burn out, that we appreciate what we've got. Neither of us takes this success for granted. But as the years go by and we're further and further away from the hard struggles we once faced, we WILL stay grounded. We WILL always look to the future while remembering our past.

And finally, a big thank you for all the continued support and custom from YOU, our beautiful Bountylicious family.

Only one thing remains to be said:

'Hell yeah!'

Our very first Charity Ball at the Chester hotel Aberdeen. Here, we raised £18K

Our second Charity Ball at Jurys Inn Aberdeen. Here, we raised £20K

Having a munch on the job. One of our fantastic winners made these just for Bounty!

Getting set up at Royal Deeside show (Boo, it's raining) but a great weekend – we even all camped in the caravan!

The Bounty Fleet all clean, outside Bounty HQ

Bounty the Guide Dog: first meeting with him as a puppy. We can't wait to see his progress

Looking over the sea at Banff (Calvin & Cobi)

Our Doberman Bo: a big part of the team keeping everyone entertained behind the camera!

Lady of the House Lola: Leanne had Lola since before her & Calvin met. She is now 10

The newest edition: Loco the Bengal. Supposed to be a mouse catcher, demoted to sofa sleeper

StoryTerrace

Ingram Content Group UK Ltd.
Milton Keynes UK
UKHW020631160623
423384UK00002B/33